WOLSUNG

SECOND EDITION

Steampunk Skirmish Game

Credits

Written by
Łukasz Perzanowski
Wojciech Chroboczyński
Jan Cieślicki

Wolsung universe created by
Artur Ganszyniec
Maciej Sabat

Produced by
Micro Art Studio

Cover art by Sławomir Maniak
Illustrations on pages (8, 58, 59, 60, 61, 63, 64, 65, 66, 70, 78, 82) by Mateusz Bielski
Illustrations on pages (56, 68, 80) by Sławomir Maniak
Illustrations on pages (71, 72, 73, 74, 75, 76, 77, 83, 84, 85, 86, 87, 88, 89, 90) by Marta Michalak
Illustration on page (62) by Rafał Cyman
Illustration on page (13) by Gunship Revolution
Ilustration on page (120) by Tod Allen Smith

Layout by Magdalena Szafran and Łukasz Perzanowski
Graphic Design by Magdalena Szafran, Rafał Bagiński and Sebastian Makowski
Miniatures sculpted by Łukasz Krysa of "Krysa Project" and Rafał Cyman
Miniatures painted by Michał Grabowy and Joanna Litwin
Terrain designed by Jan Horydowiec, painted by Łukasz Perzanowski
Photography by Michał Grabowy and Jan Cieślicki

Proofreading by
Jan Cieślicki, Jan Horydowiec, Carsten Kunz

Special thanks to:
Our Indiegogo and Kickstarter backers, Sebastian Makowski, Artur Ganszyniec, Rob Alderman, Kacper Graczyk, Piotr Kupper, Maciej Grabowy, Olaf Górak, Mateusz Stromski, Tomasz Sikora, Szymon Znosko, Szymon Rząd, Shaga, Justin McAuley

Contents

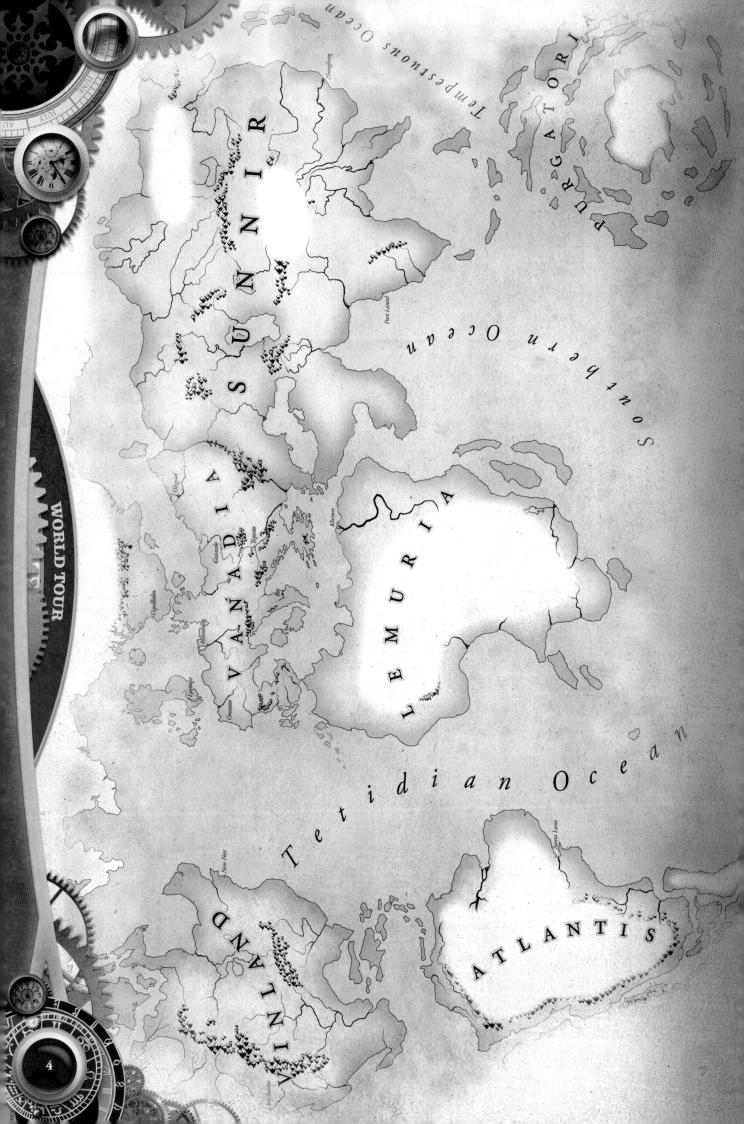

WORLD TOUR

SUNNIR

PURGATORI

VANADIA

LEMURIA

Southern Ocean

VINLAND

Tetidian Ocean

ATLANTIS

Tempestuous Ocean

World Tour

The world of Wolsung is an alternate version of our own world in the late 19th and early 20th century, strongly influenced by adventure novels, action movies, video games, and comics. It contains enough familiar elements for you to feel right at home, while also not skimping on novelty. There are plenty of surprises in store for your play sessions.

„*The world is changing rapidly. The Great War has contributed to enormous advances in science and the emergence of a new kind of magic – the Magic of Steam. The greatest of all inventions, the steam engine, has become the symbol of our brave new era.*

With the rise of giant factories, the age of mass production has begun. Cheap, high-quality products are available to everyone, not just the rich, popularizing the recent scientific achievements. Steamobiles zoom along the streets, the Metropolitan Rail network entangles the entire globe, trains riding their tracks both under- and aboveground, luxurious steamers provide comfortable cruises to overseas colonies, and the sky is filled with majestic airships. The infrastructure of great cities provides a standard of living beyond the reach of our ancestors. Gas lamps illuminate our houses, while pneumatic mail enables quick communication between any addresses in the city. Metropolises communicate via the crystalograph network.

Magic has entered universities and schools, no more a plaything for a select few, becoming a working tool of every educated person. Thanks to the work put in by geomancers, buildings of today are built in such places and using such materials that the structures' energy flow harmonizes with their purpose. As a result, hospital patients heal faster, parks provide better rest, and gaining knowledge at schools is more pleasant. Alchemists have moved out of cramped basements in favor of modern laboratories and factories. Golems are being utilized more and more extensively, and the brilliant minds of cabalists and numerologists have created the first mechanical calculating machines."

Excerpt from „Know Your Nation" – a textbook for elementary school first-graders.

Victorian Fantasy

The game world is a magic-infused version of our 19th century, in which Victorian ladies and gentlemen are derived from fantasy and mysterious magic is intertwined with amazing steam technology.

Steamobiles zoom along the streets, luxurious steamers provide cruises to overseas colonies, and majestic airships slice across the sky. Magic, hand in hand with technology, provides the world with steam golems, cabalistic counting machines, and fearsome iron dragons.

The Wolsung universe is full of challenges. Mysterious temples and wild native tribes await intrepid explorers in uncharted jungles. The undead still lurk in the sewers beneath the city – a horrifying relic of the Great War. Mad scientists and evil geniuses plot their dastardly plans.

Technology and Magic

Despite being remarkable inventions, devices created with the use of New Magic have become commonplace for the Vanadian people. Skyscrapers compete with factory chimneys in the race towards the sky in the sprawling, bustling cities. On the crowded streets, the last remaining carriages give way to shiny, noisy steamobiles. The sky is filled with majestic airships and small, agile postal wyverns. The ground is riddled with mine shafts, canals, sewer pipes, and geomantic chambers.

Seas are littered with military leviathans, transoceanic palace ships, mana extraction rigs, transport steamboats, and luxurious yachts. Even waters depths hide fewer and fewer secrets, as submersibles keep diving deeper and deeper. The railway system arrives in the colonies, followed by civilization. The world has been tamed.

Thanks to efficient postal and crystalograph services, information now circulates faster between continents than between cities in pre-War times. Gas lanterns illuminate streets and homes, and the power of steam provides heat and power to household appliances.

„I consider this omnipresent optimism to be very premature. The war has left much greater scars that the authorities are willing to admit. They seem to completely downplay the fact that an enormous stretch of Wotanian land – one along the Aquitanian border, where the greatest battles of the recent conflict took place – has been completely and irreversibly destroyed. During the final stage of the trench warfare, this area has been subjected to radiation of an intensity exceeding 700 thaums, and 20 tons of shells have been dropped per square yard! When we put the deaths of thousands of soldiers into consideration, one should not be surprised by the severe disturbances in the structure of the Astral that have permanently warped the land. Vegetation will never return to most areas, and energy flow disturbances are so enormous that even airships extend their routes by more than 100 miles in order to avoid these locations. (...)”

Excerpt from the controversial book „The Lands of Havoc” by Sir Jonathan Glimpshire

Communication

Networks of pneumatic mail (commonly called „pneuma”) cover every major city. It works by putting a capsule with the letter into a feeder. Compressed air pushes it into a system of pipes, where a complex system of switches reads the position of the capsule's serrated rings, directing the package towards the selected number. In big cites, such as Lyonesse, letters normally reach their destinations within two hours. Intercity pneuma lines are not deemed as economically viable yet.

The radio makes use of the unique properties of crystals, which start throbbing under the influence of mana, spreading the Astral's vibrations and evoking a similar effect in all nearby crystals. The limited effective range of this phenomenon, reaching only several miles, necessitates the construction of a dense network of transmission masts. Radio receivers are slightly larger than an average cupboard and require their own power supply.

The crystalograph operates on the same principle as the radio, but its purpose is long-distance communication, not entertainment. It lacks a main transmitter, and its transmission masts do not form a network, but branching lines that end with transceiver apparatuses. The message travels from station to station until it reaches a receiver, where it is automatically recorded on paper. Crystalographs are used mostly by companies, particularly newspaper agencies. Messages can also be sent and received in select post offices.

The cinema is adored in a borderline hysterical manner, and famous actors are treated as national heroes. Every backwater town tends to have some kind of projection space, even if it is just a rented out school assembly hall, the screen is nothing but a white sheet, and all the films are silent. Cinemas in metropolises are true temples of entertainment, overflowing with gold, velvet, and glistening marble. Here, the films are colored by hand and accompanied by a soundtrack recorded on perforated tapes, played on only the highest-quality speakers.

Transportation

Steamobiles are probably the most popular mode of transport today – the steam-powered vehicles have conquered the roads all over Vanadia. They are now modern and stylish vehicles, no longer the awkward pre-war horseless carriages from the past. Steamobiles are fueled by alchemically enriched coal briquettes. Before driving off, one needs to be mindful to take some time to heat up the boiler and fill up on water. Then, it is enough to keep an eye on the pressure gauge and activate the briquette feeder every once in a while by pulling the appropriate lever. A sizable network of service stations lets drivers clean out the hearth, as well as quickly replenish fuel and water. The major stations also provide all necessary repair services.

The railway is irreplaceable for long-distance journeys. Its passenger lines connect all major cities and allow to journey across Vanadia in less than two days, including stops at the stations. The comfort level varies from simple wooden benches in third class suburban lines to velvet-lined lounges in long-distance express routes.

Metropolitan Rail – due to the widely known elven sensitivity to iron, the first railway lines connecting Lyonesse with nearby towns were constructed underground. This is how the famous Underground Metropolitan Rail came to be, which has inspired many similar enterprises in other capital cities. Even today, the Alfish railway lines lead though mostly unoccupied areas, and stations are built outside the cities or in the suburbs.

Mechanical animals are a peculiar type of golems. Faster and stronger than their live counterparts, they possess a very rudimentary level of self-awareness and intelligence. In spite of that, however, they are more than capable of understanding and executing relatively complex commands and are well suited for performing tasks unfit for steamobiles. The most common mechanical animals are horses and oxen. The former are used by elite police units in most countries, while the latter are mainly utilized for farming in hard to reach areas.

Behemoths are huge, heavily armored multi-legged combat golems invented during the Great War. They are over 16 feet tall, equipped with state-of-the-art cannons, and require a crew of six to ten. Today, these golems form the core of armor divisions of almost every army in the world.

Wyverns are flying machines based on their live counterparts. Like all mechanical animals, they possess a kind of rudimentary consciousness implanted by golemologists. Quick, maneuverable and fickle, the biggest among them can accommodate even up to six passengers. Wyverns are most commonly used by courier companies for delivering express packages and mail. When an experienced pilot takes charge one of one of these machines, it turns into a deadly weapon.

Airships, thanks to air elementals trapped inside the balloons, beat the faster and more agile wyverns in terms of load capacity, range, and flight ceiling. Running between capital cities and overseas colonies, they are capable of transporting hundreds of passengers in luxury.

Lyonesse

A pearl among cities – that is how the greatest metropolis in the world is usually described. Lyonesse is located on a meander of the river Theter. Along with the suburban areas within its administrative borders, it is nearly 800 square miles in size. Lyonesse took full advantage of each and every day of its two-thousand-year-old history, becoming the greatest metropolis in the world. The river separates the illustrious palace of Queen Titania, the parliament building, and the skyscrapers in the Tintagel District from the smog-ridden slums of Bridgebank.

The capital of Alfheim is a city of universities, museums, art galleries, textile workshops, docks, ironworks, and factories. It is a center of the film industry, the last harbor for immigrants from all corners of the world, a great melting pot of religions, cultures, and cuisines. A city of commerce, art, crime, wealth, and poverty. A city of wonders. A city of contrasts. The city of cities.

The City in the Fog.

First Impressions

Newcomers from the continent will immediately notice the truly elven approach to spatial planning. Towering buildings surrounded by green gardens, parks, plazas with comfortable benches, and ponds built just to place quaint bridges over them. At least that is the case in the wealthier districts. The less representative areas are considerably more crowded and foul-smelling. Tenement houses fight for every square inch, sinking slowly into the swamplike ground.

There are four natural lakes within the city's administrative borders. The famous Astrological Observatory was built on the shores of Fishbone Lake. Many young gentlemen have taken a fondness for Lake Ferret and like to arrange their bloody duels on its shores at least once a month. Fairy Pond, in turn, starred in more movies than Eleni Blumchen and Baldwin de Rouke put together! And finally, there is the rather small Municipal Lake, which is where the annual national swimming competition takes place. Other than that, most parks are perfect for a boat trip. The Earl's Park management is proud of its crystal clear waters, and the Shangese-style ponds in College Park are famous for their oriental giant catfish. Representatives of foreign intelligence agencies traditionally hold meetings while feeding the ducks of the Aquarium – the pond in the Botanical Gardens, as seen on postcards.

Any popularity contests would probably be won by the Abbot's Gardens, picturesquely located next to Theter itself. It is here where the various cultural or sports events take place. Baroness Nimblewist's charity concerts are held in the beautiful Regency-era conservatory, with a skating rink constructed in front of it for all to enjoy. The other city parks are no less popular: the Botanical Gardens, the Royal Park, or the Lyonesse Zoo.

Let us not forget about the river dividing the city. Despite the Old Father being stitched together by nearly a dozen bridges, more than ten ferry corporations operate in Lyonesse. Dozens of Shangese junks and refitted Serenian gondolas float between Pothill, Quirinale, Jaksun Town, and Uldnesse, hauling their passengers along Theter between charming restaurants and gambling houses.

Lyonesse is the quintessential city. It has elements from Ankh Morpork, Cyberpunk's Night City, Marvel comics' New York City and, above all, Victorian London. There is no point in describing all the districts. If you feel the need for any specific kinds of scenery, amazing locales, strange communities, then simply add them in. Rest assured that they have always been there – you simply never left the metropolitan rail at that station.

The Tintagel District is the City of London, with its skyscrapers that are somewhat reminiscent of the Empire State Building. All major crimes are investigated by Alven Yard. The Fog that sometimes envelops the city is a magical phenomenon – wayward pedestrians or even entire buildings do get lost in it every now and again.

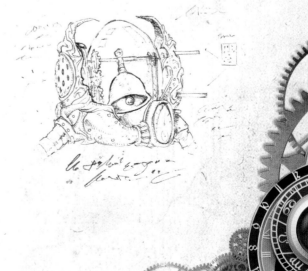

Heroes

Imperialism and progress are key words for Lyonesse-based heroes. Lyonesse is the most modern of cities and the heart of a vast colonial empire. Spending a year here is akin to visiting half the world. Growing up in Lyonesse is an experience like no other. In this city, mere street urchins witness wonders on a daily basis, wonders that would not even occur to even the most educated Wotanian citizens.

People talk constantly in Lyonesse, at any time, in all of the languages of the world. They whisper in the foggy docks, pontificate in the university auditoriums, sing over mugs of dark beer, gossip over gin and pickled eggs, testify in police stations, chat in clubs over brandy and cigars, flirt in lounges and theater loges.

They exchange opinions on whether having eleven bridges over Theter is enough or not, comment on the latest delivery of colonial goods to d'Arrots, meet up for the opening of the Museum of Golemic Figures, complain about the influx of immigrants, laugh at cartoons in the daily newspaper, and toast to the Queen's good health.

Nobody seems to talk about the hundreds of thousands homeless people, poor living conditions of laborers, curious accidents at the docks, prostitution, drunkenness, or crime among minors. Nobody comments on the fact that not even several years' worth of Alven Yard's investigations could put the stop to the Butcher of Lyonesse. Nobody stops to think whether absinthe, lotus, and laudanum are truly the best medicine against melancholy and various anxieties of urban life.

Demographics

Each year, thousands of people from Alfheim, Vanadia, the imperial colonies, and the rest of the world pack up and move to Lyonesse. The population of this melting pot of nations grows at an alarming rate and has doubled in the last century, reaching a staggering seven million inhabitants (as per data provided by the latest census). However, the amount of people staying within the capital's administrative borders during the day is nearing ten million. The additional three million consists mostly of residents of neighboring towns seeking temporary employment in the city of opportunity.

The Pearl's social diversity is incredible, truly the world in a nutshell. Dekanians, Windians, Mictlans, gnomes from Ultima Thule... Every race, every nation, every possible language is represented. Dreaming of a twelve-course Shangese-themed feast? Not a problem. An Atmanian rug? Send a pneuma to Potrhap's Colonial Goods Store on 1 Goosfare End, Kingsplace, and an obliging clerk will send your desired product by a courier within fifteen minutes. Perhaps you are in the mood for smoking some genuine Dekanian lotus? This exquisite delicacy can be found at the smoking den in Jaksun Town, a drive to which will take you no more time than is necessary to warm up your steamobile's boiler. Gnomish dancers? Dwarven strippers? The most luscious gentlemen escorts straight from Dekan? Easily found! Better worry how you are going to pay.

Everything can be found here, and I mean EVERYTHING.

Society

Here are a few social phenomena that contribute to the unique atmosphere of Lyonesse:

Elven monarchy – Alfheim is ruled mostly by elves, although members of other races are not prohibited from taking up public office. It is just that the selection criteria created by the long-lived race do not take human biology into consideration. In order to apply for public office, one must be a respected person of the „appropriate" age of ninety. This age census can be overridden only by passing several extremely difficult state exams.

Ogre Gnome Elf Dwarf Orc Halfling Human Troll

Brass and creidnallen – the elven allergy to iron has a tremendous impact on design, industry, and technology. Non-ferrous and precious metals, mother of pearl, silk, and wood are industry's favorite finishing materials, as steel or iron objects are considered plebeian. For the very same reason the iron railway runs its routes away from noble mansions, and the Metropolitan Rail in the capital is hidden deep underground.

Empty chairs – elves do not die of old age. This simple fact turns the law of succession upside down and complicates the formal status of several public offices. Many young noblemen are not the lawful owners of their estates, but only „manage" them on behalf of their Dreaming parents or grandparents. Chairs in many offices are signed with names of employees being absent for hundreds of years – various assistants and attorneys-in-fact being used as their „temporary" replacements.

Buried alive – grand elven mausoleums in the Kingsplace Green cemetery feature bells that can be activated from the inside. This is used in case any of the elder Dreamers wake up. This is fashionable to the point where even non-elven eccentrics have bells installed in their coffins, just in case. Rumor has it that some of the bells are inactive, as there are some families who are not too keen on meeting their dear old Dreamer relatives again.

Nanny for life – elven girls from rich families are fed by wet nurses, often along with human girls, who are destined to become their companions. Humans mature much more quickly, so when the elf learns how to walk, her milk-sister can watch over her by becoming her governess. When the miss starts school, her confidante is already an adult and able to take care for her ward's education, shifting her role from teacher to chaperone as years go by. When the young elven lady is ready to be introduced into high society, her human companion retires.

Big brothers – ogres born into wealthy families are usually illegitimate and are quickly removed from the public eye. Disowned by their families, they are cut off from any sort of inheritance. Halflings are exceptions here – every child born to a halfling mother is considered a halfling. Even though the little one grows to be a nearly seven-feet-tall giant, to his family he is a brother and cousin, and woe unto anyone who has any objections.

Hat and gloves – the pale complexion of the elves as well as the dwarven sensitivity to the sun has only reinforced the belief that civilized people ought to keep their bodies covered. If conditions allow, ladies and gentlemen tend to wear hats, be buttoned up to the neck, and take off their gloves only during meals. Nudity befits only savages.

The hidden world of servants – an efficient household requires at least a dozen servants. Nobody even notices this in a well-managed house. Servants have their own entrance, narrow service corridors run inside the walls

connecting the kitchen with individual rooms, and there are doors hidden behind illusions that allow the servants to change the owner's sheets during his or her absence. A competent majordomo can program golems, and a qualified head maid knows the spells to control the house sprites. Liveries enchanted with invisibility and trays imbued with rudimentary levitation spells also prove useful during grander receptions.

Districts of Lyonesse

Historical Lyonesse

Here lies the true heart of the Empire: Uldnesse, Queenston and Uldport with the Isle of Dogs. These are the oldest districts of the city. The Queen's palace as well as the Parliament and government buildings are surrounded by streets, squares, and parks. Everything here is Alfish to the very core: the five o'clock tea, lukewarm beer in pubs, red pneuma booths, quaint squares with benches, carriages, nice and even lawns, and the polite, subtly contemptuous distance with which the locals look at the rest of the world.

Why visit this district?

Uldnesse, Queenston, and Uldport consist of museums, unique monuments, pubs, restaurants, colonial stores, charming squares, but also the most important institutions of the Empire. Every resident, tourist, or extraordinary hero will easily find an excuse not only to visit this district, but to never leave it.

Who can be found in the streets

Members of the Ash and Oak Club, monocled gentlemen in bowler hats, governesses with their wards, mounted police, newsboys, shoeshiners, florists, diplomats, traveling salesmen, tourists from the continent, newcomers from the provinces, servants from the colonies, young ladies with their chaperones, liveried butlers, government officials.

Pothill

Beyond the distinctive red lacquered gates, there lies a completely different world. The colorful lanterns, the banners flapping in the wind covered with spidery writing, the fires burning under the woks, the enigmatic smiles on the locals' faces – everything clearly points to the fact that one has entered Shangtown. This

is the district of shadow theater, dragon parades, jade figurines, beautiful tattoos, and the most incomprehensible opera in the world.

Why visit this district?

Pothill offers experiences unattainable anywhere else in this hemisphere. Only here one can have century-old wyvern eggs for lunch, get an enchanted tattoo, bet on dog and basilisk fights, visit a massage parlor or a black lotus smoking den, enjoy the sensual services of the best brothel in the city, learn the art of kung-fu and origami, or purchase a miniature bansai tree.

Who can be found in the streets

Rickshaw drivers, monks in saffron robes, geishas, porters in black pajamas, wise men with long beards and even longer nails, elderly mantis breeders, empty-eyed lotus smokers, ghostly black-haired girls, blind street musicians.

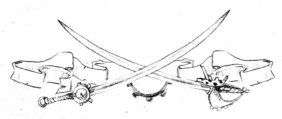

Quirinale

Visitors are welcomed with rows upon rows of market stalls full of colorful, fragrant fruits and vegetables, clay vats with olives, and fish and seafood spread over crushed ice. Quaint restaurants lay their tables with checkered tablecloth and lure potential customers with the smell of spaghetti and minestrone. In Little Scylla, even dull Alfish houses look as if they were longing after the sunny south. This is a good place. Just remember not to bother any halflings wearing trenchcoats and fedoras.

Why visit this district?

Going out for a meal here every now and again is definitely recommended, as few things can compare to Donna Fumadore's homemade lasagna, or grilled calamari found in the Vendetta family's trattoria. One could also visit here with more risky goals in mind: to seek allies for some less than legal business, investors interested in bold endeavors, or someone who would be willing to avenge some real or imagined injustice in exchange for a favor.

Who can be found in the streets

Servants carrying baskets full of pasta and fruit, cooks covered in flour, loud-mouthed fishwives waving smoked eels around, ogre porters, young halflings with killer mustaches and tipped hats, fresh corpses in the side streets.

Stableton

When the sun is nowhere to be seen, despite it being noon, it means that you came upon Stableton. The district is eternally shrouded in a veil of black, acrid smoke coming from dozens of smelters, factories, rolling mills, forges, and workshops. The streets wind their way between pipelines and conveyor belts, houses cower beneath the brick chimneys and fiery mouths of blast furnaces. The cobblestones tremble to the rhythm of the giant machines. This is the dream of New Magic put into practice.

Why visit this district?

Stableton is the district of invention and industry. It is here where people develop new technologies, test amazing machines, seek investors and partners for bold enterprises, and build laboratories and workshops. Crimes are routinely committed in the name of new technologies, plans get lost or change owners, and horrible accidents happen even to the most careful. As if that were not enough, at least one new mad genius tends to emerge from the smoke of Stableton each month.

Who can be found in the streets

Laborers, forge golems, scrap collectors, automatic trains, unloaded steamobiles, inventors, elven investors in airtight golemic litters, children playing in the slag heaps, drunk gremlins, geniuses of crime, saboteurs.

Svart Thule

There is a separate, mysterious world hidden in the shadows of the District's modern skyscrapers. Upon taking just a few steps, the atmosphere shifts rapidly. Shop signs written in runes, godi clad in black and red, silent silhouettes of golems, streets populated mainly by gnomes, the constant clatter of difference engines coming from office windows, houses numbered according to some kind of insane logic – everything here communicates the following to the visitor: „you are a stranger here."

Why visit this district?

Svart Thule attracts visitors with secrets and specialized knowledge. Only here one can seek advice from the wise godi, or the difference engines. Specialists of many exotic fields can be found here, including experts on custom-made golems, rune magic, cabalism, long-forgotten legends, and rare branches of the occult. Other then that, the best accounting, insurance, and brokerage offices are to be found right here.

Who can be found in the streets

One-eyed godi in ritual robes, hunched old women with their goats, tailors, officials with tech-abacuses and ink-stained sleeves, giant clay golems, tiny mechanical golems, merchants, traveling salesmen, and lots and lots of gnomes.

Tintagel District

Majestic pediments made of sandstone, granite and marble, towering skyscrapers with windows made of Seren crystal, streets meticulously planned out by geomancers, multiple alleys and squares – it all adds up to a sublime symphony of modern, urban magic. An unending crowd of officials and the rich pours along the wide sidewalks and cobweb bridges that bind the towering buildings together. Here, in the heart of the world's high finance, fortunes are made and lost.

Why visit this district?
Simple – for money. In the District, one can find sponsors willing to invest in even the wildest expeditions and most insane research. Doing so would not necessarily require legal means. Bank vaults and millionaires' collections await daring burglars. And where, if not here, could one run a truly spectacular scam?

Who can be found in the streets
Officials, newsboys, messengers and couriers, hectic secretaries, ogre gatekeepers, redheaded heads of supervisory boards, millionaires in limousines, lost investors, white-collar thieves, ruthless con artists, elven heirs, brokers, accountants.

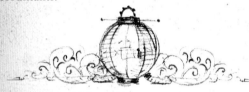

Windbog

The picturesque Lyonesse skyline is perfectly visible from the gentle hills of the Ferret Forest. Somewhere down the river, the District's skyscrapers, Stableton's chimneys, and the lonely Tall Tom emerge from the Fog and smog. But that does not matter here. In Windbog, the sun is always shining, the sky is forever blue, and the grass is greener. Between a game of golf and a hot air balloon flight, this is where one can finally unwind.

Why visit this district?
Windbog offers an excuse to finally loosen up the corsets and stiff collars, and shout away all the frustration that the frantic 19th century inflicts on the anxious heroes. This is the perfect place for duels, turbulent affairs, bets over vast fortunes, and testing the latest in vehicle technology.

Who can be found in the streets
Gentlemen in linen suits and straw hats, ladies in horse riding gear, ogres with golf clubs, gnomes wearing aviator scarves and hats with goggles, elven maidens with tennis rackets, children in sailor outfits jumping rope, young men in racing steamobiles, couples on tandem bicycles, maidens riding unicorns.

Other Interesting Places

Treecoven – the royal astrological observatory is located in the suburbs, exactly on the prime meridian. This makes the place particularly suitable for performing magic rituals.

Comedians End – the part of Uldnesse (the Old Town) known for its cabarets, pubs, and theaters, the most famous among which is the Hand and Mask pub, stuck in between two no less popular theaters that are locked in a customary rivalry with each other: New and Moon.

Ethnic districts – in Lyonesse, immigrants prefer to stick together. Everyone knows that Svart Thule is a gnomish ghetto, Jaksun Town is inhabited by immigrants from Dekan, dwarves from the continent live in the old Stableton factories, and Quirinale, famous for its halfling restaurants, is openly called Little Scylla, just as Pothill is called Shang Town.

Clairvale – this wealthiest, most luxurious district dominated by the aristocracy is full of mansions, lavish gardens, wide streets, secret love affairs, scandals, addictions, and far-reaching eccentricity. All it lacks is anything made of iron.

In the Fog

The famous Lyonesse Fog is a phenomenon that is unique on a global scale. Although it has accompanied the city since time immemorial, no one has yet been able to formulate a coherent theory that could explain all the aspects of this anomaly. There have been suspicions that the Fog is a physical manifestation of the Astral's ephemeral matter intruding the real world. This theory lacks concrete proof, however.

The Fog tends to haunt Bridgebank the most, but its appearances are by no means limited to just this single district. Although Theter's right bank is usually more prone to foggy weather, the Fog tends to envelop the entire city at least once a year, its range extending to Bellville and Ferret Forest. These episodes can last anywhere from just an hour to even three full days.

The SUC

Hidden in the bowels of Lyonesse, there lies a machine built out of hundreds of linked difference engines. They call it the Subsystem of Ultrafast Calculations, and it is truly one of the greatest inventions of our time. And, according to skeptics, also one of the most alarming ones.

The Machine Hive

The SUC is located in an indistinct building in between Svart Thule and the Tintagel District. Narrow hallways, winding staircases, and tiny, document-filled offices entangle the mechanical core of the structure. The SUC occupies the entire eight-story-high central hall and several basement floors. The building is riddled with crankshafts, switches, gears, conveyor belts, and pneuma tubes. When the Machine needs to be expanded, walls are demolished, closets moved, and employees resettled.

The constant, unrelenting, maddening clatter of gears and whizzing of transmission belts reaches all the corners of the building. Mana discharges that power data transfer pipelines emit rhythmic thuds from below ground, as if beats of a giant's heart. Ventilation machines alternate between sucking up air into the structure and releasing hot steam outside. The building resembles a giant anthill, where official-looking termites bustle around the enormous bulk of a mechanical queen.

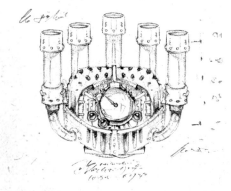

The Subsystem's technical maintenance is performed by top engineer-cabalists from Svart Thule, who are mostly avid iterationists. Their work involves the efficient removal of mechanical defects, replacement of worn parts, and supervision over the inevitable reconstruction processes. Specialized, self-iterating differential algorithms have been commissioned to design the machine's modules. This means the the SUK has been expanding by itself for about three years, without anyone's control, following a plan only it knows.

Mechanical Bureaucracy

The Subsystem of Ultrafast Calculations appeared of nowhere. No one remembers when the linked differential engines suddenly started working as a unified, efficient organism. The SUK collects the citizens' personal information, facilitates the operation of dozens of minor public offices, and processes data from tax returns, the land registry, the civil registry office, and more. Simply put, it is a vital part of municipal bureaucracy.

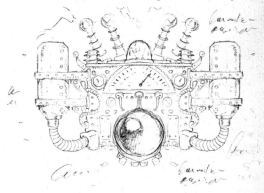

An army of officials keeps feeding thousands of miles of perforated tape into the Machine, analyzing the mysterious hole patterns on the celluloid sheets, making decisions that affect the lives of millions of Lyonesse citizens.

The SUC's influence grows with each passing day. The automatic semaphore system that is currently being tested in the Tintagel District is doing great at managing traffic, and it is only a matter of time before the entire city is covered by it. The SUC has been composing timetables for the Metropolitan Rail Supervisory Commission for months now. The Lyonesse stock market is fully reliant on the Machine to provide the necessary financial calculations. Alven Yard is warming up to the idea of having a centralized national criminal database. Golemic ravens venture farther and farther away from Svart Thule. On the SUC's behalf, they watch Lyonesse from above, providing the Machine with a constant stream of information.

Thank goodness that the SUC is merely a huge, cold, unthinking machine, built only to closely adhere to the Cabalists' commands. Right?

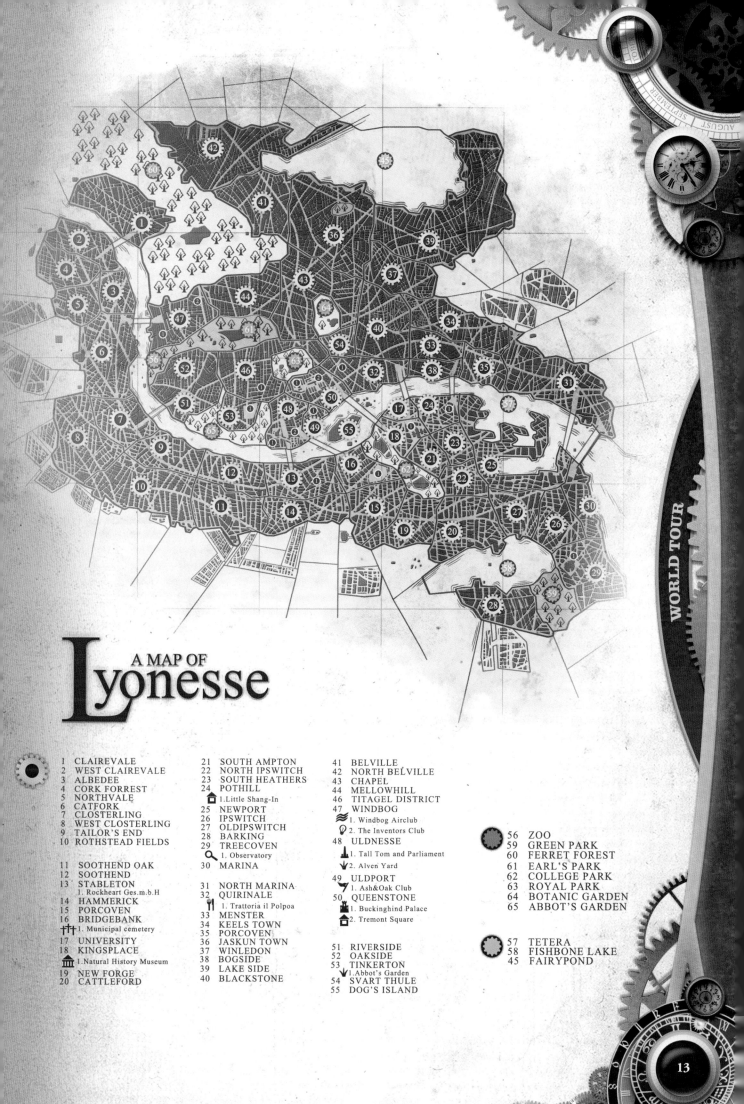

A MAP OF Lyonesse

1	CLAIREVALE	21	SOUTH AMPTON	41	BELVILLE	
2	WEST CLAIREVALE	22	NORTH IPSWITCH	42	NORTH BELVILLE	
3	ALBEDEE	23	SOUTH HEATHERS	43	CHAPEL	
4	CORK FORREST	24	POTHILL	44	MELLOWHILL	
5	NORTHVALE		1. Little Shang-In	46	TITAGEL DISTRICT	
6	CATFORK	25	NEWPORT	47	WINDBOG	
7	CLOSTERLING	26	IPSWITCH		1. Windbog Airclub	
8	WEST CLOSTERLING	27	OLDIPSWITCH		2. The Inventors Club	
9	TAILOR'S END	28	BARKING	48	ULDNESSE	
10	ROTHSTEAD FIELDS	29	TREECOVEN		1. Tall Tom and Parliament	56	ZOO
			1. Observatory		2. Alven Yard	59	GREEN PARK
11	SOOTHEND OAK	30	MARINA	49	ULDPORT	60	FERRET FORREST
12	SOOTHEND				1. Ash&Oak Club	61	EARL'S PARK
13	STABLETON	31	NORTH MARINA	50	QUEENSTONE	62	COLLEGE PARK
	1. Rockheart Ges.m.b.H	32	QUIRINALE		1. Buckinghind Palace	63	ROYAL PARK
14	HAMMERICK		1. Trattoria il Polpoa		2. Tremont Square	64	BOTANIC GARDEN
15	PORCOVEN	33	MENSTER			65	ABBOT'S GARDEN
16	BRIDGEBANK	34	KEELS TOWN				
	1. Municipal cemetery	35	PORCOVEN				
17	UNIVERSITY	36	JASKUN TOWN	51	RIVERSIDE		
18	KINGSPLACE	37	WINLEDON	52	OAKSIDE		
	1. Natural History Museum	38	BOGSIDE	53	TINKERTON	57	TETERA
19	NEW FORGE	39	LAKE SIDE		1. Abbot's Garden	58	FISHBONE LAKE
20	CATTLEFORD	40	BLACKSTONE	54	SVART THULE	45	FAIRYPOND
				55	DOG'S ISLAND		

WORLD TOUR

13

What is Wolsung SSG?

The Wolsung Steampunk Skirmish Game is a miniature combat game, where clubs of extraordinary ladies and gentlemen, as well as shadowy organizations and agents of obscure powers, solve their disputes by blade and gunshot rather than discussion. Each game represents a point where paths of two or more such clubs cross, while they work on the same goal, but for opposite purposes. As such, the careful deduction and data gathering as well as social meetings that led them to this point are left for Wolsung Roleplay narrative; A game of Wolsung Skirmish represents the point where the outcome is decided by a keen eye, reflexes and a bit of luck.

Basic terms

Player: You. The person controlling the Models.

Allied Player: An Opponent who decides to help you in achieving the Scenario Victory Conditions. This may be decided by the Scenario or by negotiations during the game. In a 2 Player game there may be no Allied Player.

Opponent: Every other Player than you.

This means that an Allied Player is always also an Opponent.

D6: A six-sided die with sides numbered from 1 to 6.

Success: A D6 roll of 4, 5 or 6.

1. The dice on the left are Successes. The dice on the right are not.

Test: When a test is required, you need to roll a number of dice equal to the Characteristic the test calls for, and compare the number of successes either to a set number (Static Test) or another Player's number of successes (Comparative Test)

Static Test: Any test that has a set difficulty number [x]. In order to succeed you need to achieve an equal number or more successes than the number in brackets.

Comparative Test: Most of the time Players will be asked to make Comparative Tests. Both the attacking and defending Player will test the required Characteristic of their Model. In order for the Active Model to succeed it needs to achieve an equal number or more successes than the number achieved by the Target Model.

Critical Hit: Successes over the required amount. See Damage, page 27.

Re-roll: A re-roll enables you to roll dice again. There are two types of re-rolls in Wolsung:

A **test re-roll:** For example, Beginner's Luck. All or none of the dice rolled have to be rolled again.

A **die re-roll:** For example, Master Gunner. A number of dice can be rolled again.

In any case the result of the re-roll must be accepted even if it's worse than the initial roll. You cannot re-roll dice that have already been re-rolled.

Measuring Distances: Distances between Models are measured in three dimensions. When checking the distance between Models, measure from the nearest edge of each Model's base. Distance to Objects is measured to their closest external point, because they don't have bases.

Pre-measuring is allowed: you can check all distances at any time. For example, prior to declaring any Action.

Measuring Movement: It is important to note that movement, unlike everything else, is measured in two dimensions, ignoring the vertical distance for the most part. When checking the distance for movement, measure "from front to front" of the Model's base. A Model may not move vertically up or down more than its basic Move in inches unless Jumping or Falling.

Model: A Model is a physical representation of a character in Wolsung SSG. Heroes and Henchmen Models are always mounted on a base and any distances from or to a Model are measured to the nearest edge of its base.

Active Model: A Model that is currently making an Activation or Action.

This Model: A Model that is subject to the rule in question.

Friendly Model: A Model controlled by the Player or his or her Allied Player.

Enemy Model: A Model controlled by an Opponent.

Attacker: The Active Model or Object that is making an Attack against the Target.

Target: A Model or Object that is chosen as a Target of a Spell, Melee Attack or Ranged Attack, or Special Ability.

Living Model: All Models are Living Models unless described otherwise.

Non-Living Model: Models with this rule are not living, and therefore are not affected by effects which are applied to living Models only. Furthermore, LoS cannot be drawn to Non-Living Models in Deep Water. (Examples of Non-Living Models: Golems, Undead).

Object: A category for Vehicles, Devices, Objectives. These do not need to be mounted on a base - in this case all the distances to them are measured to their closest external point. If targeted with a Spell, a Ranged or Melee attack, they have a set Defensive Difficulty (DEF) that needs to be at least equalled to hit them.

DEF [x]: (DEFensive difficulty) This is the difficulty of a Static Test that an attacker needs to at least equal in order to succeed. It can apply to a Ranged Attack, Melee Attack or a Spell - a corresponding characteristic will be used by the Attacking Model.

For example, if a Device has a DEF [1] it means that the Attacker needs at least one Success to hit it.

Range: A distance in inches.

Terrain: See Terrain, page 36.

Elevated Terrain: See Elevation, page 37.

Base to Base contact (BtB): In order for the Models to be in BtB contact, the edge of the Model's base needs to contact another Model's base edge or its base vertical projection up to the height of the top of the Model's head.

Line of Sight (LoS): An unobstructed straight line from one Model's head to any portion of another Model's body (ignoring weapons, hats, umbrellas, mechanical accessories and bases). Models have 360° field of vision. Models can draw LoS through their and other models' bases.

Within: A Model is within Range, Template or Terrain if at least a portion of its base overlaps with the Range, Template or Terrain.

Completely Within: A Model is completely within Range, Template or Terrain if its whole base overlaps with the Range, Template or Terrain.

Template: An area of effect of a certain size and height, represented by a suitable marker. See Special Rules, page 55.

1. Top left model is in BtB with the Fire Template but it is not within it. Top right model is within Smoke Template. Bottom left model is completely within Acid Template. Bottom right model is completely within Mist Template.

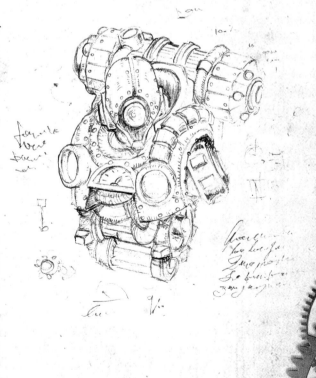

RULES

Model Characteristics

Models are either Heroes or Henchmen.

Heroes are extraordinary individuals with unique abilities and gadgets and are best compared to Player characters in a role playing game.

Henchmen are the common folk, servants, minions, and ordinary people that somehow ended up working with Heroes. They do not possess any Heroic capabilities but come by the dozen.

Each Hero or Henchman Model is described with a profile, listing all of its characteristics in a following order:

	Actions	Move	Fight	Str	Guns	Reflex	Wounds	
Butler HENCHMAN Human / 30mm	2	5	2	3	2	3	9	1

A – Actions: The Model is allowed to perform up to this number of various in-game Actions such as Move, Shoot etc. in its Activation.

M – Move: An amount of inches the Model may move per Action spent.

F – Fight: The close combat ability of the Model. This is the number of dice rolled both to hit and defend in melee.

S – Strength: The physical strength of the Model. This is the amount of Damage the Model inflicts in melee each time it hits.

G – Guns: Ranged weapon handling skill. This is the number of dice rolled to hit with a ranged weapon.

R – Reflex: Agility of the Model. This is the number of dice rolled to avoid various dangerous situations, such as being hit from afar.

W – Wounds: The amount of damage the Model may suffer before it is killed. When a Model is reduced to 0 W it is removed from the battlefield.

Single letter abbreviations are used throughout these rules. A capital letter always means the corresponding characteristic, for example if a Model is asked to make a R test it means it is asked to make a Reflex Test, rolling a number of dice equal to its Reflex characteristic.

Cards

In Wolsung SSG playing cards are used for a number of purposes. The card value is only used for the purpose of Stealing Initiative or Delaying Activations. Bridge card value is used (for example, 9 is higher than 8), with Ace being higher than the court cards. If cards of equal values are played, then their suit is the tie-breaker and is used in the following order:

1. Spades.

2. Hearts.

3. Diamonds.

4. Clubs.

Aside from Stealing Initiative or Delaying Activations, the cards may be discarded to allow Hero Models make Heroic Actions.

If you choose to use Jokers, treat them as a lowest card of any suit (decide which suit as the card is played).

Activation

In Wolsung SSG Players alternate moving and acting with their Models, one Model at a time, in each game turn. Moving and/or acting with a Model is called This Model's Activation. Each Model can be Activated only once every game turn.

Action

Action: Every Model has a number of Actions, (usually 2) at their disposal each Activation. Once a Model is Activated, it can do a number of things equal to the number of its Actions in any order the Player pleases.

For example, a Model can move and then shoot, shoot and then move, move twice, or remain in place and shoot twice, provided it has 2 Actions on its Characteristic Profile.

Types of Action

• **[Action]:** The Model performs the chosen Action.

• **[Quick Action]:** The Model can make a Move and then performs the chosen Action.

That Action's type remains the same. (For example, Cast a Spell Action is still a Cast a Spell Action and not a Move Action.) This is important because of the restrictions on which Actions you are allowed to perform while in melee. Also, you cannot make more than one Quick Action per Action.

Possible Actions

• **Move [Action]:** Move up to the Models M Characteristic in inches.

• **Charge [Quick Action]:** Move into BtB Contact with an enemy Model and then perform a Fight [Action].

• **Fight [Action]:** Make a melee attack against an enemy Model in BtB.

• **Shoot [Action]:** Shoot an enemy Model in LoS and Range.

• **Cast a spell [Quick Action]:** Apply a spell effect to one or more Target Models.

• **Special [Action] or [Quick Action]:** Some Models have their own special Actions. If an Ability has an [Action] or [Quick Action] next to its name, you have to spend an Action to use it.

A model may be required to make a Static or Comparative Test when making certain Actions. If a Model is allowed to target more than one Model in an Action, all Targets need to be declared before any tests are made.

Whenever there is more than one Model allowed to be Activated at the same time, make all the Actions of one of these Models before making any Actions of the other Model(s).

At the end of the Action, apply all the effects in the following order:

1. **Special effects** *(for example, a weapon disabling a gadget).*

2. **Healing.**

3. **Damage.**

Game Turn

Game turn sequence

1. **Start of the turn**
    1.1. Start of the Turn Effects
    1.2 Drawing Cards
2. **Activations**
    2.1. Stealing the Initiative
    2.2. Model Activations
    2.3. Delaying Activations
3. **Surplus Activations**
4. **End of the turn**
    4.1. End of Turn Effects
    4.2. Effects expiration

1. Start of the turn

1.1 Start of the Turn Effects

Game effects, abilities and special rules can happen at the start of the turn. These Effects are applied in this step.

1.2 Drawing Cards

Each Player draws a number of cards based on the size of the game (see Size of the game chart, page 40) and combines them with their existing hand of cards. The Player then discards cards down to the maximum number. The maximum number of cards a Player can keep is based on the game size.

For example, in a 3 Hero game at the beginning of each turn each Player draws 6 cards and then discards cards until he has 6 of them. This enables Players to keep some better cards from previous turn, filter their hand or change the strategy.

2. Activations

2.1 Stealing the Initiative

In some occasions it may be worthy to Activate more than one of your Models directly after one another.

There are two types of stealing the Initiative:

Option 1: **Stealing the First Player's Initiative.**

This is done <u>directly before the First Player Activates his first Model this turn</u>. Each Player willing to have the Initiative may choose one of the cards in his hand and place it face down on the table in a clockwise order. Reveal the cards. The Player with the highest card is the First Player in this and following game turns and may now Activate his first Model this turn. The Initiative is passed to the next Opponent in a clockwise order.

1. One Player initiates by playing a card face down.

2. The other player also plays a card face down. Both are revealed simultaneously.

3. The Player on the right won and gets to Activate a model.

Option 2: **Additional Activation.**

A Player who has any Mindless Models still left to Activate may not opt for Additional Activation.

Just after you Activated one of your Models and before passing the Initiative to your next Opponent you may try to Activate an additional Model. In order to do so, choose one of the cards in your hand and place it face down on the table. Then your Opponent(s) may either try to counter this Action or allow it (pass) in a clockwise order. If they are not willing to give you the chance of another Activation they also choose a card from their hand and place it face down on the table. Reveal the cards. If your card is higher than all of the Opponents', you are allowed to Activate another Model. Otherwise the Initiative is passed to the next Opponent. It is possible to perform this Action several times in a row if you have enough cards in your hand.

1. The Player on the right initiates by playing a card face down.

1. The left Player wins so the right Player does not get to Activate another model and the initiative proceeds as normal.

2.2 Model Activation

In this Step Players alternate to Activate Models as follows:

The First Player chooses one of his Models and performs a number of Actions with this Model. Then the Initiative is passed to the next Player. Each Model can only be Activated once in a game turn. The Initiative is passed around by the Players until all but one Player run out of Models that can be Activated this turn. Any surplus Models the other Player might have left to Activate yet are Activated in the Surplus Activations.

2.3 Delaying Activation

In some occasions it may be worthy to wait with your Model's Activation.

A Player who has any Mindless Models still left to Activate may not Delay Activations.

This is done directly after the Initiative is passed to you. In this case you also have to repeat the process above, see 2.1 Stealing the Initiative. The difference is that if you win the card comparison you may force your Opponent (in case of 3+ Player games a previous Player) to Activate another Model before passing the Initiative to you. It is possible to perform this Action several times in a row if you have enough cards on your hand.

1. The left Player tries to force the right Player to Activate another model.

2. The right Player has played the lower King and loses this bid. He is now forced to Activate another model if able.

3. Surplus Activations

If only one Player has more Models left to Activate, they are Activated one at a time in the order decided by the Player until there are no more Models to Activate this turn.

4. The end of the turn

4.1 End of Turn Effects

A part where some effects occur, listed by various special rules.

4.2 Effects expiration

In this moment all effects with the "Until end of turn" rule expire.

All Templates are removed from the battlefield at the end of turn unless noted otherwise.

Movement

Move: [Action]

Move the Model up to its Movement value in inches. A Model may never move through enemy Models unless specifically stated but it may move through your own Models. The Model cannot end its Movement in a place where there is no room for the Model's base or in BtB with an enemy Model (unless it makes a Charge).

Moving as a part of a [Quick Action]:

When a Model performs a Quick Action always complete the movement before starting the actual Action.

The distance a model moves and the route it chooses is modified by Terrain (See Terrain, page 36).

Shooting

If a Model has a ranged Weapon, it can perform a Shoot Action. The Model needs Line of Sight (LoS) to the Model he or she wants to target.

An example of a ranged weapon's profile:

Name	S	0-8"	8-16"	16-24"	Notes
Pistol	4	+1	-1	-2	Quick

Name: Name of the Weapon

S: Strength of the Weapon

Range columns:

0-8", 8-16", 16-24": If the Target is in this range, apply the given modifier to the Guns Test

Notes: Abilities of the Weapon

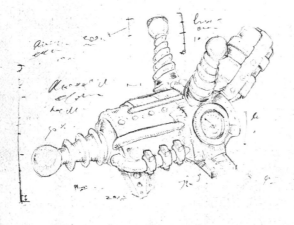

How to shoot a target?

1. **Check LoS and Range**, as premeasuring is allowed. If the Target is not in Range you may choose another Target.

2. **Choose a Target Model.**

3. **Target Model chooses a Reaction:**

   • **Hold Nerves:** The Model's status remains unchanged.

   • **Dive for Cover:** The Model immediately becomes Toppled.

4. **Roll the dice:**

   The Active Model rolls a number of dice equal to its Guns modified as follows:

   • Weapon's Range modifiers.

   • Weapon's special rules.

   • Elevation bonus.

   The Target Model rolls a number of dice equal to its Reflex modified as follows:

   • Elevation bonus.

   • Cover.

If the Active Model scores an equal or higher number of successes as the Target Model, the shot hits and damage is applied to the target. Otherwise it's a miss.

1. Shooting Model rolls 2 successes versus Target Model's 2 successes: A Hit!

3. The model on the right is in Cover [1] and receives one more Reflex die when targeted with a ranged weapon.

2. Shooting Model rolls 1 success verus Target Model's 2 successes: A Miss!

4. The model behind the box on the left is in Cover [2]. The Golem model in the middle has no Cover. The Lab Assistant behind some crates to the right is in Cover [1].

Weapon's Range modifiers: Check the distance between the shooting and Target Model. Look at the columns in Ranged Weapon's profile. If the Model is closer or equal to the range in the first column after the weapon's name, apply the bonus from this column. If not, move to the second column and do the same. If the distance is larger than the distance written in the last range column, the shot automatically misses.

Cover [x]: The number is a positive modifier to a Model's Reflex value. When the Model's body is partially obscured from Line of Sight (LoS), it gets Cover [1]. That means that the Target Model gains an additional Die to its Reflex Test.

When the Target Model's body is obscured more than 50% from Line of Sight (LoS), it gets Cover [2]. Some specific special rules may change the way cover is applied to some Models.

Toppled: A Toppled Model gains a Reflex bonus of 2 against shooting attacks. The drawback is that a Toppled Model has its Fight reduced to 1 and can only choose to Fence in melee. A Toppled Model remains so until it Activates. It MUST spend its first Action of the next Activation to stand up. It cannot do anything other than standing up in that Action.

5. The model on the right is Toppled and gains 2 additional Reflex dice when targeted with a ranged weapon. This does stack with Cover.

Elevation bonus

• A Model benefits from +1G when targeting a Model on a lower elevation (at least 3").

• A Model benefits from +1R when targeted by a Model on a lower elevation (at least 3").

1. The Butler is Elevated against the Golem. The Shade is Elevated against both the Butler and the Golem.

The Butler in the middle benefits from both bonuses against the Golem at the bottom and neither against the Shadow at the top.

Shooting into melee

It is possible to shoot at an enemy Model in BtB with a friendly Model. However, there is a chance of hitting the friendly Model! Make the shooting attack as normal, but roll for the Reflex of the Target Model and every Model in BtB with it. The Model that rolls the least number of successes is the final target. If there is more than one Model with the least number of successes, the owner of the Active Model decides which one of them is the target.

If the active Model scores at least an equal number of successes than the Model in Melee with the least Reflex successes that Model is hit and damage is applied.

If there is a Model on larger base involved in a melee, all Models on smaller bases involved gain +1R for avoiding being shot within this melee.

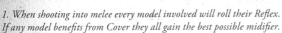

1. When shooting into melee every model involved will roll their Reflex. If any model benefits from Cover they all gain the best possible midifier.

2. Every model mounted on a smaller base will gain one additional die to their Reflex.

Melee

When a Model is in melee (BtB contact with an enemy Model) it may only perform a Move or Fight Action. Models may Move out of melee as per Leaving Melee, but they may not move into melee with enemy Models in the same Action.

1. These models are in BtB and as such in melee.

Charge: [Quick Action] The Model must enter BtB with an enemy Model. As a part of the Charge, the active Model may make one Fight [Action] in addition to moving. When in melee, Models may not use the Charge Action.

Note there is no LoS required at the start of the Charge Action.

2. Charge!

Fight: [Action] A Model makes a melee attack against an enemy Model in BtB contact.

A Model may elect not to attack in either a Charge or Fight Action. In case of a Charge, the Model only moves into BtB with the target enemy Model, in case of a Fight Action the Model does nothing. No dice are rolled and no cards may be played.

How to fight in melee?

1. **Choose a target in BtB**

2. **Attack:**

   2.1. **Defender chooses a Reaction:**

   - **Fence:** The Model fights normally.

   - **Parry:** The defending Model gains +2F in this Action, but cannot deal damage itself.

   If a Model is not allowed to choose any of these options, the Model gains no bonuses: neither the bonus F for Parry, nor the chance to damage the Attacking Model for Fence.

   For example: If a Model is Toppled and attacked by an Elf.

3. **Roll the dice:**

   Both Models roll a number of dice equal to their Fight modified as follows:

   - Weapon's and Model's special rules.

   - Bonus for Multiple Combat.

   - Melee Elevation Bonus.

If the Attacking Model scores an equal or higher number of successes as the Target Model, the strike hits and damage is applied to the Target.

Otherwise, if the defending Model has chosen the Fence Reaction, the damage is applied to the Attacker. If the Defender chose to Parry no damage is dealt.

Fighting a melee on different elevations

Models may engage in melee with Models on higher or lower levels. If there is not enough room at the other level due to enemy Models blocking it, a Model may still perform a Charge Action, provided it has enough Move to reach BtB contact with the Model. Place both Models as close to BtB (using normal Movement rules) contact as possible. They count as being in BtB and in melee with each other.

Models may engage in melee and/or be engaged if the base of the Model standing higher is on the same level as the base, legs, torso or head of the Model standing lower.

Melee Elevation Bonus

Models at least 1" higher up gain +1F

If a Charge Action starts at least 3" above the Target the charging Model benefits from +1F this Action.

3. This charge will not gain a melee elevation bonus as the Ogre Bruiser does not start it at least 3" above the Phoenix.

It is possible to get +2 total elevation bonus, if a Model starts a Charge Action at least 3" above the Target Model and is placed in BtB with it so that it is at least 1" higher up.

1. These models are in BtB and the Ogre Bruiser gains +1F melee elevation bonus.

2. These models are not in BtB as the base of the Ogre Bruiser is higher than the top of Pheonix's head.

Multiple Combat

If a Model is in BtB with more than one enemy Model, it is engaged in a melee with all of them. A Model can only choose one Model as a target of their Fight Action, unless noted otherwise. A friendly Model in the same melee as the Active Model, mounted on a base no smaller than the enemy Model, provides a positive modifier to each other friendly Model in this melee equal to its Fight value, both in friendly and enemy Activation. If a Model enters BtB with an enemy Model who is already in BtB with another friendly Model, the above rules apply immediately.

More than 1 Model from each side

If there is already a melee with 2 Models from one side and 1 from the other side, as soon as a second Model from the other side enters the same melee, the combat is split up. One Model from each side is set aside half an inch in BtB with each other, so that no more than one Player has multiple Models in any of the melees. The Player who has the Initiative decides which Models to move and how to split the melee.

1. The Ogre Bruiser (Fight 4) is helped by the Butler (Fight 2) so will roll a total of 6 dice against the Golem's Fight of 3.

2. The Butler will not help the Ogre Bruiser against a Security Golem as it is mounted on a larger base.

3&4. The Ogre Bruiser has both of the enemy models in range and has a choice of who to engage.

RULES

It is possible for a Model to engage 2 Models in BtB at once, if its Move distance allows it. Again, the Player who has the Initiative decides which Models to move and how to split the melee, but at least one enemy Model must remain in BtB with any other friendly Model who was already in BtB with enemy Models at the start of the Activation.

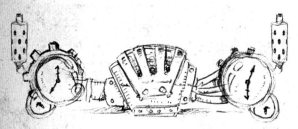

1. *The Player controlling the Ogre Bruiser can engage both of the models he can reach simultaneously if he or she chooses.*

Leaving melee

It is possible for a Model to leave BtB contact with enemy Model(s). The leaving Model has to perform a Move Action. At the Start of that Move Action the leaving Model has to make a comparative Test of its Reflex against the highest Fight Value of the enemy Models in this melee. Heroic Deeds may be made by both sides using black cards. If the Model wishing to move from combat rolled at least equal to the number of Successes as their enemy (after modifications from Heroic Deeds), it may move from the combat as normal. If it rolled less Successes, then it must stay in combat and the Action is lost.

2. *The Phoenix will need to roll his Reflex of 5 against the highest of the opponent's Fight values, in this case the Ogre Bruiser's Fight of 4.*

Damage

When a Model is hit by a ranged, melee or magic attack it suffers damage equal to the Strength of the Weapon, Model or Spell modified by:

- Armor.

- Critical hits.

Damage: This is the number of Wounds a Target Model loses when hit with an attack. It is equal to Strength of the Weapon, Model or Spell plus the number of Critical Hits minus the Target's Armor.

Armor[x]: This number is a negative modifier to any Damage a Model receives.

Critical Hit: Every success the Attacking Model rolls over the number of successes rolled by the Target Model. Each Critical Hit modifies the damage the Target Model suffers by +1.

3. *Mary Fearless rolls 3 successes to hit with her Strength 4 Colt Navy, 2 more than Thorvald rolls for his Reflex. She gains 2 Critical Hits in this attack, modifying the Strength by +2, for a hit with a Damage 6 in total!*

Magic

Magic is not readily available at every moment in Wolsung SSG. A magical power requires tedious preparations, meditation, visiting places of power, or harnessing the power of raw elements. All of these takes much more time than could be represented during a skirmish game. Therefore, only a small number of Models are capable of using Magic and casting Spells.

Magic Ability [x]: This ability allows the Model to cast spells. The [x] defines the number of dice the Model uses for casting spells.

Magic Ability will also have a **Magic Type** defined, which will only come into effect when using Nexus [x]: Magic Type.

Nexus [x]: Magic Type: Models with a Magic Ability [Magic Type] within 6" of a Model or Object with this rule gain +x to Magic Ability.

A Hero created using the Character Creation Rules may have more than one Magic Ability characteristic. Each Spell comes with its own Magic Ability and represents the number of dice the Hero uses for casting this Spell.

Each Spell is described by a set of parameters:

• **Name**

• **Type**: The spells are divided into Magic Projectiles, Magic Attacks, Buffs and Auras.

• **Cost**: Indicates what card you have to discard to cast this spell;

0 – no cards

1 – any card in Hero's suit

2 – Court Card in Hero's suit, Ace in Hero's suit or two cards in Hero's suit

• **Range**: Maximum Range in inches of the spell.

• **Strength** or S: Magic Projectile Spells only, determines their damage.

• **Description**: Includes special rules of the spell.

Cast a Spell: [Quick Action]. Each time a Model wants to cast a spell, you must discard cards in the Model's suit as indicated by the spell's cost. The spells are organized into 2 categories, each with 2 subtypes.

Magic Projectile and Magic Attack spells

Magic Attacks and Magic Projectiles are spells that can only target enemy Models.

If it was a Magic Attack spell, apply the effects written in the Description of the spell to the Target Model.

> **How to cast a Magic Projectile or Magic Attack spells?**
>
> 1. **Choose a Target in range and LoS.**
>
> 2. **Pay the cost.**
>
> 3. **Roll the dice:**
>
>   • **The Active Model** rolls a number of dice equal to its Magic Ability.
>
>   • **The Target Model** rolls a number of dice equal to its Reflex (may be modified by special rules).
>
>   • If the Active Model scores an **equal to or higher** number of successes as the Target Model, the spell hits the target.

1. Magic Attack or Projectile spell. The casting model paid the cost. The models make a Comparative Test of Magic Ability vs Reflex.

If the spell cast was a **Magic Projectile** spell, apply Damage as normal equal to spell's Strength modified by Armor and Critical Hits.

Magic Aura and Magic Buff spells

Magic Buffs [x] and Magic Auras [x] are spells that target one or more Models according to the spell's description.

X is the spell's Difficulty.

How to cast a Magic Aura of Magic Buff Spell?

1. **Choose Target(s) in range and LoS**

2. **Pay the cost**

3. **Roll the dice:**

   - **The Active Model** rolls a number of dice equal to its Magic Ability.

   - If the Active Model scores a number of successes **equal to or higher** than the spell's **Difficulty,** the spell succeeds and its effects are applied.

When Choosing a Target with **Magic Aura[x]**, you target every Model that is eligible target (specified in the spell's description) in the spell's Range and Active Model's LoS.

When casting a **Magic Buff[x]** spell you may only choose one friendly model as the Target.

1. Magic Aura. The casting model paid the cost and made a Magic Ability test. Two models are in range as indicated by green arrows. One model is out of range as indicated by an orange arrow.

2. Magic Buff. The casting model paid the cost and made a Magic Ability test. One friendly model in range is chosen as the target.

Heroes

All the Hero Models in Wolsung SSG have special rules that reflect their supernatural strengths and great powers. These rules are common to every Hero Model.

Hero only characteristics

Suit: Every Hero has its specific suit, one of the card suits (Spades, Hearts, Diamonds or Clubs). Only cards in the Model's suit may be used for Heroic Movement and Heroic Recovery.

Funds: Funds reflect a Model's wealth, contacts, or other connections. The number is added to the Club's Fund Pool, which may be used to buy Henchmen before each game.

1. One whole Suit of cards: Hearts.

Hero special Rules

Heroic Recovery: At the start of the Hero Model's Activation, if it's Toppled you may discard a card in the Hero's suit to stand up instead of spending an Action.

Heroic Move: At the start of the Hero Model's Activation you may discard a card in the Hero's suit. If you do, until the end of Activation This Model is allowed to treat all Rough Ground as Open Ground and to make special Move Actions (that can be combined with other Quick Actions):

Climb: The Hero Model may move vertically, up to the number of inches equal to its M up, or any number of inches down. He may not move through the floors of other elevations and there must be space to place the Model at the end of the movement. He must end the move as close horizontally to his starting position as possible. It means he may Move up to his basic Move in inches through Open and Rough Gound to be in base contact with the wall he intends to climb and end this Action in base contact with the climbed wall, no higher up than his basic Move.

1. Heroic Climb. The Hero can Move to BtB with the climbed surface first. It is then placed with BtB with the climbed surface up to its Movement higher.

Jump: The Hero Model may move horizontally up to the distance of its M in inches ignoring any terrain that is up to 2" high. His movement may not end in a place that is more than 2" higher than this starting location. It means that a Hero can jump from a building to building, ignoring the gap between them.

1. Heroic Jump. The Hero can move up to 2" up and any distance down.

Heroic Swimming: This works exactly as Heroic Move: Models moving Heroically through Deep or Shallow water treat it as Open Ground. They are still Toppled if they are hit while in the water and have to test for Drowing.

Heroic Deed: Players may discard a card to add a number of successes to the test for Shooting, Melee, Casting or Activating Objectives, after the roll is made.

Only **black cards** may be used for Melee, Leaving Melee and Casting Buffs or Auras on friendly Models.

2. Black Cards.

Only **red cards** may be used for Shooting and Casting Magic Projectiles and Magic Attacks or Auras on enemy Models.

Only cards in the Hero's suit may be discarded for Activating Objectives.

3. Red Cards.

Court Cards and Aces add +2 successes to the test. Other cards add +1 success.

4. Red Court Cards.

If both fighting Models are Heroes, they will either use black cards both or red cards both as specified above. The first Model to use the Heroic Deed is the Model who has rolled the least successes, or in the case of tie, the Target Model.

The Model's controller discards one eligible card face up, adding the corresponding number of successes to the test. Then the opposing Player may discard one card in the same manner. The Players take turns discarding the cards until one of them passes. The other Player may continue discarding cards until he or she passes too. The final number of successes of each Model is calculated and the attack is resolved.

Example:

John controls Mary Fearless, and Luke controls Thorvald Nielsgaard. Mary shoots Thorvald with Guns of 4, rolling 4 dice and scoring 1 Success. Thorvald uses his Reflex of 3, rolling 3 dice and scoring 3 Successes. John decides to discard a red card to add 1 success to Mary's test. Now it's Luke's turn to decide whether to discard a card and he passes, since Mary's result is still not good enough to hit Thorvald. Now John may discard any number of red cards to boost Mary's test even further. Luke however may not discard any more cards to boost the test since he already passed.

1. Mary rolled poorly. She discards a red card, but it is still not enough to hit. Thorvald passes.

2. Mary discards another red card, turning this shot into a hit! Thorvald cannot do anything as he already passed.

3. Mary could have discarded a court cart in the first place and turn this miss into a hit, but this could have made Thorvald defend with cards too.

4. The only limit to the amount of cards discarded is the number of cards in your hand. Here Mary shows a total overkill, 11 Critical Hits, 8 of which are from the discarded cards.

5. The Heroic Deed can also be used in defence. Thorvald discards a red court card. Still a hit. If Mary passes now she can not add any more cards to this test.

6. Thorvald discards another red card. Now the shot is a miss!

Funds and Cost

All Hero Models have a number of Funds ranging from 0 to 6. Funds are used to buy Henchmen Models before every game.

Every Henchman Model has a Cost you have to pay with your Funds in order to hire them. You cannot spend more Funds than the Heroes you chose have in total.

At the start of the game you cannot have more Henchmen than twice the number of your Heroes (Unless special rules state otherwise).

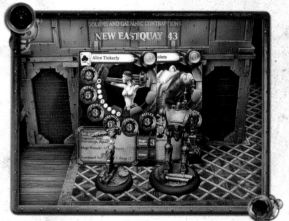

2. ...Two Lab Assistants and a Clockwork Servant.

1. Alice Tinkerly has 3 Funds. By herself she can bring to the game: A Laboratory Golem and a Lab Assistant...

3. ...Or just one mighty Security Golem.

Mundane Jumping and Climbing

It is possible for Heroes and Henchmen Models to try and cross Impassable obstacles in a mundane, if tiring and dangerous way.

A Hero or Henchmen Model may try to make a Mundane Climb or Jump Action in the following way:

Mundane Climb

Climb: [Quick Action]: Make a Reflex test with a Difficulty equal to the height of the climbed wall in inches, rounding fractions down. Friendly Models in BtB with both the climbing Model and the climbed wall add a number of dice equal to their basic Strength to this test. A Model may not climb higher than its basic Move value in inches.

If the climbing Model scores **equal or more** successes than the difficulty of the test it is placed in BtB with the climbed wall up to the climbed level.

If the climbing Model **fails** to score enough successes, it is placed Toppled in BtB with the climbed wall at the level it started.

1. *The Butler Moves to BtB with the wall and Makes a Reflex test with a Difficulty equal to the height of the wall. In the unlikely event of passing this test he is placed on top of the wall directly over the spot he was in BtB with.*

2. *In the more likely event of the Butler failing this Reflex test, he is Toppled in the spot he was in BtB with the wall.*

Hero Models may discard cards in their suit to boost this roll, but they are better off Climbing Heroically anyways!

Example 1: Climbing.

A Butler wants to climb a 3" wall. Since with his Reflex of 3 he's only just able to do it if he's lucky, he moves next to an Ogre Bruiser standing in BtB with this wall and asks for a lift up. The Ogre Bruiser gives him a boost, and the Butler needs to make a Reflex test with a difficulty of 3, rolling 10 dice - his Reflex of 3 and the Ogre Bruiser's Strength of 7 - he rolls 5 successes as the Ogre Bruiser launches him into the air, and is now on top of the wall.

3. *A friendly Ogre Bruiser gives the Butler a lift up, adding his Strength to the Reflex test the Butler makes. With such muscle it is much easier to pass the test.*

Mundane Jump

Jump [Action]: Make a Move test with a Difficulty equal to the total distance jumped in inches (measured diagonally if there is a difference in levels), rounding fractions down. If the Model lands on an elevated terrain but within 1" of its edge, make a Falling test.

If the jumping Model scores **equal or more** successes than the difficulty of the Jump test it is placed in the chosen spot. A Model may not end this Action more than 1" higher than it started. A Model may not attempt to Jump a distance longer horizontally than its basic Move in inches.

If the jumping Model scores **less** successes than the difficulty of the jump, it Falls down and is placed Toppled a number of inches along its jump route equal to the number of successes rolled and suffers Fall Damage.

1. The same Butler now stands before a problem of dismounting the wall on the other side. He makes a Jump Action, trying to make a leap to a ground level about 2" from the base of the wall. The measured distance to this place is just over 3,6" (since the wall itself is 3" tall) so he now needs to make a Move test with a difficulty of 3 (as the fractions are rounded down) - his basic Move is 5, so he rolls 5 dice, needing to score at least 3 successes. He rolls 3 successes, so he makes the jump safely and is placed at the spot he wanted to; 2 inches from the base of the wall.

2. This time the Butler only rolls 2 successes, so he ends up right about the place he wanted, but is Toppled and suffers Fall Damage of 3 - a nasty concussion or a sprained ankle!

Hero Models may discard cards in their suit to boost this roll, but they're better off Jumping Heroically anyways!

3. The Butler wants to jump down one level from the roof of a warehouse onto another building's roof. He makes a Jump Action, picking a spot just far away to clear the gap but also behind a raised edge of the roof.

He now needs to make a Move test with a difficulty of 3 due to the distance. His basic Move is 5, so he rolls 5 dice, needing to score 3 successes to land where he wants. He rolls 3 successes so jumps down safely and is placed where he wanted. This place however is within 1" of the edge of the roof, which is still elevated from the ground. He now needs to make a Falling test. If he fails either the Jump test or falling test he will be placed Toppled on the level below directly below the spot he was jumping to or falling from and will suffer Fall Damage.

Terrain

Terrain: Everything that is not Models or Objects. The Models and Objects are allowed to be positioned on and interact with Terrain to gain advantage to Line of Sight, Elevation, Cover, etc. No Model or Object may be positioned in a way that would be unstable. Models may not move through spaces narrower than 1/2" for 30mm Base Size, 1" for 40mm Base Size, 2" for any other Base Sizes. If an Object is capable of moving, it may not move through openings it would not physically fit through. Models and Objects need to finish each Action in a stable and allowed location.

Open Ground

Models and some Objects move up to their Move characteristic value in inches in each Action they spend moving over **Open Ground.** Most of the surface of the playing area will usually be an Open Ground - grass, dirt, cobblestones, low hedges and walls, barrels and crates of up to 1" height and 1" across.

1. Models may move up to their full Move each Action over Open Ground.

Rough Ground

Models may move up to half of their Move characteristic in inches horizontally for each Action they spend moving over **Rough Ground.** Terrain features such as ruins, walls, barrels and crates of over 1" height and 1" across but no more than 3" high are Rough Ground. This represents the Model moving vertically in addition to horizontal movement.

2. Models may move up to half of their Move each Action in Rough Ground.

Impassable Ground

Walls, enclosed buildings and terrain features higher than 3" should usually be classified as **Impassable Ground.** Normally Models may not pass through them (unless climbing, jumping or using Heroic Move).

3. The wall and building behind the Ogre Bruiser are Impassable ground. The shack to the right is Rough Ground.

Elevation

Models and some Objects may enter levels higher or lower than 3" via **ladders** by moving as in Rough Ground, or **stairs** by moving as in Open Ground. There must be room for a Model's base at the end of the access point. Note that Model's vertical movement distance may not be greater than its base Movement value in inches. Elevation provides bonuses to Models on it. (see Shooting and Melee).

Elevated Terrain: Any Terrain higher than 3".

Water

Water may be either Deep or Shallow (defined by the scenario or Players before the game).

Shallow Water is Rough Ground for all Models.

Living Models hit by an attack while in Shallow Water are Toppled in addition to any Damage they suffer.

Deep Water is Rough Ground for all Models.

Non-living Models in Deep Water have LoS to them blocked as they simply walk on the bottom.

Living Models that are hit by an attack while in Deep Water are Toppled in addition to any Damage they suffer.

Living Models Toppled in Deep Water must test for Drowning.

Drowning: A living Model Toppled in Deep Water must roll a number of dice equal to the number of the Wounds it is missing from its starting number of Wounds plus its Armor at the start of its Activation. For every die that is not a success it loses 1 Wound, ignoring Armor.

A Hero Model can use the Heroic Recovery Ability to ignore Drowning.

Doors

Doors may be in 3 states: Open, Closed and Locked.

Open Doors: Open Doors can be freely moved through as a part of a Move or Charge or other Quick Action and count as Open Ground for Models whose base size can move through an opening of this size. If a Model's base size is too large it cannot move through. A LoS can be drawn through an Open door. They can also be closed as a Quick Action and are treated as Closed Doors until they are opened again.

Closed Doors: Models cannot Move, Charge or move as part of other Quick Action through Closed Doors. No LoS can be drawn through. Closed Doors can be opened as a Quick Action and are treated as Open Doors until they are closed again.

Locked Doors: Models cannot Move, Charge or move as part of other Quick Action through Locked Doors. No LoS can be drawn through. Locked Doors can be unlocked as an Action with a **Reflex** or **Strength** test with a set difficulty. The Locked Doors may have a difficulty of [1], [2] or [3], depending on their sturdiness and complexity of the lock. Clearly define the difficulty of any Locked Doors before the game.

If the Model unlocking the doors rolls equal or more successes than the difficulty of the lock, the door is Unlocked. If the Model rolls fewer successes than the difficulty of the lock, the door remains Locked.

Doors Unlocked with a Reflex test are treated as a Closed Doors and can be Locked again as an Action with a Reflex test with the same difficulty it had before.

Doors Unlocked with a Strength test are treated as Open Doors and cannot be Locked again.

1. Some models are not apt at picking locks.

2. Forcing a door will leave it permanently open.

Falling

If a Model is hit with a ranged, magic or melee attack or becomes Toppled while within 1" of an edge of an elevated terrain it is on, make a Reflex test with a difficulty of [2] to see if the Model **Falls Down.**

A banister or a similar raised surround within 1" of the testing Model changes the difficulty of this test to [1]. If the barrier is at least 1" tall then it also provides a +2 Reflex bonus; if it is less than 1" tall it provides a +1 Reflex bonus.

If a Model rolls at least the number of successes equal to the test's difficulty it remains where it was. Otherwise it Falls Down. Hero Models may discard a card in their suit to pass this test.

> **Fall Down:** The Model falls down from the edge it is closest to if there is more than one edge within 1". Place the fallen Model Toppled on the lower level directly below the point it fell from.

> **Fall Damage:** The fallen Model suffers a hit with a Strength equal to the height it fell in inches, rounding fractions down and ignoring Armor.

If the falling Model's base would overlap a base of any other Model on the lower level, each of these Models has to make a Reflex test against the Strength of the falling Model. If they roll more successes than the falling Model they jump to the side and are unharmed - move the Models so they are no longer in BtB with any other Model. If the falling Model rolls equal or more successes they are hit, Toppled and suffer Crush Damage. The hit may cause Critical Hits. The falling Model is placed Toppled in BtB with them.

> **Crush Damage:** When a Model is hit by a falling Model it suffers damage equal to the total height it fell from, rounding fractions down and modified as follows:
>
> • Armor
>
> • Critical hits

Hero Models may discard red cards to boost the Reflex to jump out of the way.

Hero Models may NOT discard cards to boost Strength to hit other Models harder with their own falling body.

Example:

A Triad Phoenix manages to balance himself on top of a shack on the roof of a two-storey building. He gets hit with a ranged attack and has to make a Reflex test or Fall Down. He rolls 4 dice (just his Reflex, no banister here!), needing to score 2 successes. He fails and Falls Down straight on top of the unsuspecting Shadow (as he was closer to the edge above the Shadow than to the one overlooking the edge of the building), who now has to test its Reflex against Phoenix's Strength to see if he manages to clear the area in time. The Shade rolls 4 dice and the Phoenix rolls 7 dice, getting 2 and 3 successes respectively. The Phoenix tumbles down and hits the Shade. The Phoenix suffers 2 Damage ignoring Armor (1 for every full inch he fell) and is placed Toppled in BtB with the Shade, who suffers 3 Damage (1 for every full inch of the fall plus one Critical Hit) and is also Toppled.

Now both of them have to test their Reflex again to see if they Fall Down further as they both became Toppled within 1" of an edge of an Elevated terrain. This time the difficulty is only [1] as there is a banister around the roof, but it is not high enough to provide them with the +2 Reflex bonus.

Playing the game

In order to play, you'll need at least two Players, each controlling a number of miniatures forming a club, a flat surface of roughly 3ft by 3ft (36"x36"), several six-sided gaming dice (D6), a standard, 52 playing cards deck, a measuring device and some terrain to represent the surroundings of particular scenarios.

Size of the game

Duel	1 Hero per Player	Learning Game	4 cards per turn
Clash	2 Heroes per Player	Starter Game	5 cards per turn
Brawl	3 Heroes per Player	Basic Game	6 cards per turn
Combat	4 Heroes per Player	Full Game	7 cards per turn
Encounter	5 Heroes per Player	Expanded Game	8 cards per turn
Battle	6 Heroes per Player	Epic Game	9 cards per turn

Every Player chooses an equal number of Heroes depending on the size of the game. During a campaign or tournament, a roster is only required to list the Heroes the Player will use. Heroes have a playing card symbol representing their Suit on their cards.

Example

Players agree to play a campaign, using 4 Heroes each. The first game they play is a Brawl, so each of them picks 3 Heroes for this game out of the 4 in their roster.

Before the game

1. Decide on the size of the game
2. Pick a Scenario
3. Deploy Terrain and Objectives
4. Pick your Heroes
5. Reveal Heroes
6. Spend your Funds on Henchmen
7. Draw cards
8. Determine First Player
9. Choose Deployment Zones

1. Decide on the size of the game

Agree with your Opponents on the game size, by choosing how many Heroes each Player controls.

2. Pick a Scenario

Scenarios make the gameplay more exciting, as they add more depth to the game, and Players have to adjust their strategies to accomplish the mission objectives. See the Scenarios section for detailed information.

3. Deploy Terrain and Objectives

When placing terrain on the battlefield, there are several things to consider:

- At least 50% of the battlefield should be covered in terrain features.

- At least 50% of these should be Elevated Terrain (Buildings, walkways, etc. at least 3" tall).

- Placing Elevated Terrain on the edges of the Battlefield will make any shooting Models totally dominate the game. Placing Elevated Terrain mostly at the center of the battlefield makes for a more interesting game. The Elevated Terrain should block some movement paths, but at the same time form alternative routes to be explored by the Models with Heroic Move ability.

- There should be numerous Access Points (stairs, ladders) to allow every Model to access at least some portions of Elevated Terrain. Not every Elevated terrain should be easily accessible.

Some Scenarios instruct you to place Objectives which can be Activated by Models. See Scenarios for more information.

4. Pick your Heroes

Each Player now secretly chooses a number of Heroes allowed for the size of the game from the Heroes available to their club.

5. Reveal Heroes

The Players now reveal the chosen Heroes to each other simultaneously.

6. Spend Funds on Henchmen

Add together the Funds of all chosen Heroes. You can hire Henchmen with a total cost of the added Funds your Heroes provide. The maximum number of Henchmen is double the amount of Heroes you use.

7. Draw Cards

At the start of the game, each Player draws a number of Cards from the deck that equals your number of Heroes +3.

For example:

You and your Opponent agree on a Brawl with 3 Heroes per Player. So each Player draws 6 cards.

If you run out of cards, shuffle the discarded cards pile and form a new deck to draw from as soon as you draw the last card.

Remember: You draw cards in Before the Game step 7: Draw Cards, and at the start of the first game turn in step 1.2 Drawing Cards (see page 18) again. You will have to discard cards down to the maximum number based on the game size at the start of your first game turn, which means you begin your game with a well-balanced hand of cards. Choose them wisely!

8. Determine First Player

Each Player has to bid for being the First Player by playing a card face down from their hand. Reveal those cards. Then each Player may play additional cards face down until they pass or run out of cards. Reveal the additional played cards. Highest card wins (see Cards, page 16) and the Player who played it is the First Player and will choose the Deployment Zone, deploy the Models on the battlefield and will choose a Model to Activate first each turn. The other Players then deploy Models in a clockwise order.

9. Choose Deployment Zones

2 Player Deployment Zones

In a 2 Player game, the Player who is the First Player gets to pick the Deployment Zone from the ones listed below. The Players then deploy their whole Clubs, starting with the First Player, unless the chosen Deployment Zone states otherwise.

• The opposite sides of the battlefield, up to 6" from the edge.

• The opposite quarters of the battlefield, no closer than 12" to the middle of the battlefield.

• The opposite corners and two adjacent edges of the battlefield, the Models are placed touching these edges at the start of their first Activation.

The following Deployment Zones may be chosen with the Opponent's consent. They are a lot of fun but start the action on the first turn, and may be more tactically demanding.

• The Players alternate placing Models, starting with the First Player. Hero Models need to be deployed first, no closer than 12" from any other Hero. Henchmen Model next, no closer than 6" from any other Model. Models that have special deployment rules may opt not to use them.

• One Player chooses a building and deploys all Models inside and on top of it, the other Player deploys no closer than 6" from it. The building has to be within 12" from the center of the table and be at least 6"x3".

Multiplayer Deployment Zones

In a 3 or more Players game the Deployment Zones are chosen in a clockwise order, starting with the first Player. No edge, corner or building may be chosen by more than one Player. When there is more than one Player to deploy at one time, start with the First Player or Player whose position in initiative is the closest to the First Player.

• A point in the middle of the edge of the battlefield. This Player's Models have to be deployed within 12" of the chosen point. This Player deploys first.

• A corner and two adjacent edges of the battlefield. This Player does not place any Models at the start of the game. The Models are placed touching these edges at the start of their first Activation instead.

• The Whole Battlefield. The Players who have chosen this Deployment Zone alternate placing Models, starting with the First Player. Hero Models need to be deployed first, no closer than 12" from any other Hero. Henchmen Model next, no closer than 6" from any other Model. Models that have special deployment rules may opt not to use them. This Player deploys last.

• One chosen building, no closer than 6" to any edge. This Player's all Models have to be placed inside and on top of the chosen building. This Player deploys second.

The Deployment Zones may change according to the scenario you choose. See the scenario section for more information.

Pothill

Quirinale

Stableton

Scenarios

A **Scenario** is where the most fun can be had from a wargame. Presented here are two sets of rules for scenarios Basic and Advanced. While the basic scenarios are enough to give you a balanced gaming experience, the fun starts when you take the tools presented in the form of the advanced scenarios and use them to build your own storytelling narrative!

Wolsung is not only about Heroes hitting themselves on the head, it is also full of daring chases, exploration in the name of science, desperate last stands and magnificent inventions changing hands. Use the Models in your collection as the Objectives for your games, allow the Player controlling an Objective to use its special rule you devised, make the Players battle in a crowded market, engage in a cloak-and-dagger assassination attempts during an embassy ball, or run from a flood caused by a migration of a rare species of vermin through Lyonesse sewers.

Basic scenarios

These are great to learn the rules of the game and Clubs.

Assassination! In broad daylight:

Victory Conditions:

• Each Player openly picks one of his Hero Models. This Model is worth 2 Victory Points to the enemy. All other Heroes are worth 1 Victory Point each.

• At the end of the game, the Player earns Victory Points for every enemy Hero Model killed.

Start of the game: Bid for the First Player as normal.

Deployment zones: Decided by the First Player.

Game length: The game lasts 3 turns.

Winning: A Player who has the most Victory Points at the end of the 3rd turn is the winner.

Assassination! Confused shady killers:

Victory Conditions:

• Each Player secretly assigns Victory Points to his Models in ascending order. The First Model is worth 1 VP, the second 2 VP, the third 3 VP, and so on. Note these values for use at the end of the game.

• At the end of the game, the Player earns Victory Points for every enemy Hero Model killed.

Start of the game: Bid for the First Player as normal.

Deployment zones: Decided by the First Player.

Game length: The game lasts 3 turns.

Winning: A Player who has the most Victory Points at the end of the 3rd turn is the winner.

Assassination! Shady business:

Victory Conditions:

• Each Player secretly picks one of his Hero Models. This Model is worth 2 Victory Points to the enemy. Note which Model it is for use at the end of the game. All other Heroes are worth 1 Objective Point each.

• At the end of the game, the Player earns Victory Points for every enemy Hero Model killed.

Start of the game: Bid for the First Player as normal.

Deployment zones: Decided by the First Player.

Game length: The game lasts 3 turns.

Winning: A Player who has the most Victory Points at the end of the 3rd turn is the winner.

Assassination! Very Important Person:

Victory Conditions:

• Each Player secretly assigns Victory Points to his Models in ascending order. The First Model is worth 1 VP, the second 2 VP, the third 3 VP, and so on. Note these values for use at the end of the game.

• Each Player openly states which of his Models is worth the most Victory Points.

• At the end of the game, the Player earns Victory Points for every enemy Hero Model killed.

Start of the game: Bid for the First Player as normal.

Deployment zones: Decided by the First Player.

Game length: The game lasts 3 turns.

Winning: A Player who has the most Victory Points at the end of the 3rd turn is the winner.

Advanced scenarios

Advanced scenario rules will enhance your gaming experience of Wolsung SSG by introduction of Activated Objectives of various types.

The following scenarios are just suggestions of how many and which objectives should be used. Use these rules to create your own scenarios that picture the particular adventure you devise.

The presented set of scenarios is suggested for tournament play, subject to modifications by tournament organisers.

Activating Objectives: In order to Activate a scenario Objective, a Model has to be within 3" and LoS of it. The Model needs to score enough successes to equal or beat the Objective Difficulty. Hero Models may make Heroic Deed by using cards in their suit to add successes to the roll. Activating Objectives is a Quick Action.

Objective Difficulty is a value in brackets next to each Objective in a description of a scenario. It may also be a value the Objective is worth at specified time unless stated otherwise in the scenario description.

An Objective has to be Activated separately by every Player.

While within 3" and LoS to the Objective Hero Models roll 2 dice and Henchmen roll 1 die for Activating the Objective. For every friendly Hero Model within 3" and LoS to the Objective add 2 dice to the roll. For every friendly Henchman Model within 3" and LoS to the Objective add 1 die to the roll. These numbers may be modified by the Objectives' special rules.

The size and shape of the Objective markers: Objective markers are **Objects** and should be modeled in a way that shows best what they represent in a scenario. This could be a heap of packages, mysterious machinery or a silent golem. They should not be less than 25mm or greater than 60mm in diameter. Objectives block LoS as a normal Object would.

Placing Objectives: The Objectives are given a definite spot to be placed on in each scenario, however they may be placed on different elevation levels if Players choose so. Therefore, Players alternate placing the Objectives, allowing every Player a degree of control on the elevation of certain Objectives. When there is an odd number of Objectives to place, the Player who placed an Objective first also places the last Objective.

Feel free to experiment with Objectives placement. Our suggestions are based on gameplay testing but may not necessarily fit with your storyline!

Types of Objectives:

Switch: Remains Active for the last Player that Activated it.

Stack: After Activation remains Active for the Player until the end of the game.

Depletable: It may be Activated only once.

Scoring Objectives: The Victory Points a Player scores for the Objectives he or she controls may be calculated at the end of every game turn or at the end of the game. Alternatively, a different Sudden Death victory condition may be used. This should be clearly defined in the scenario description.

Last Chance: This rule applies only in a game of three or more Players. After the last game turn is finished, any Player may begin a bid in order to add one more turn to the game. The Players discard cards face down in the same manner as when Determining the First Player (see page 43). Then the winner of the bid chooses to either end the game or start the final game turn. The winner becomes the First Player during this final turn.

Size of the table:

The standard size of the table is 36" by 36". There is nothing stopping you from playing on either a much larger or much smaller area though. Smaller area does not require much modification apart from a denser terrain. For every 12" any dimension of the table is larger than the standard add one more game turn and add one to the size of the game. So if a recommended size of the game on a 36"x36" table is Brawl or Combat (3 or 4 Heroes), a 48"x48" table would call for a 4-turn Encounter (5 Heroes) and a 48"x72" table would require a 6-turn War (7 Heroes).

Below are a few ready to play scenarios created with these rules. These scenarios can be mixed and matched with the Basis scenarios. Feel free to experiment with assigning different Victory Points value to Objectives.

For example, you could play a scenario where there is a central Objective worth 3 Victory Points that is not Activatable but simply controlled by whoever has the most models within 3" at the end of the game, 4 Activatable Objectives: Switch[1] worth 1 VP each positioned so that they are 9" from to closest table edges. On top of that, every enemy Hero killed is worth 2 Victory Points and every enemy Henchman killed is worth 1 Victory Point.

Svart Thule Nexus

Struggle to control a vital Nexus has entered its last stage. All the preparations are complete, the only thing that remains to be done is to adjust receivers, feed the energy elemental and synchronise flux capacitors. The nexus will then provide us with unlimited power! Unless the opposition manages to do this all first...

Before Deployment: Players alternate placing 4 Activated Objectives [2], Stack, 9" from adjacent table edges. Place a single Activated Objective [4], Switch, in the middle of the table, on the ground level. This can be Activated only by a Player who has Activated 3 other Objectives.

Nexus: The middle objective is Nexus [2] for all magic types once Activated.

Start of the game: Bid for the First Player as normal.

Deployment zones: Decided by the First Player.

Game length: The game lasts up to 4 turns.

Winning: A Player who controls the middle Objective for 3 whole Activations (own and Opponent's) or at the end of the 4th turn is the winner.

An Objective is not controlled by the whole duration of the Activation in which it is Activated.

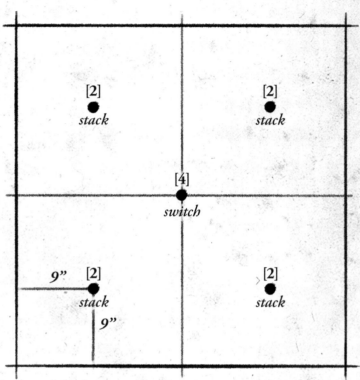

Example:
Player A Activates the middle Objective. He will need to control it for 3 consecutive Activations to win. If Player B Activates the middle Objective in the 3rd of these Activations, a new count begins from the next Activation.

Quirinale Zeppelin

The famous Zeppelin pilot McOskey has finally agreed to engage in our little venture! That is, if we can provide him with the safe landing spot in the middle of Quirinale! This requires us to signal to him from several different places as he descends! Let's just hope nobody directs him to the other fellows!

Before Deployment: Players alternate placing 4 Activated Objectives [3], Switch, 6" from table edges and 12" from the middle of the table. Place a single Activated Objective [3], Switch, in the middle of the table.

Enemy Models within 3" of an objective reduce the number of dice for Activating Objectives, one die per enemy Model.

Start of the game: Bid for the First Player as normal.

Deployment zones: Decided by the First Player.

Game length: The game lasts 4 turns. Last Chance.

Winning: A Player who controls 3 Objectives at the end of the last game turn is the winner.

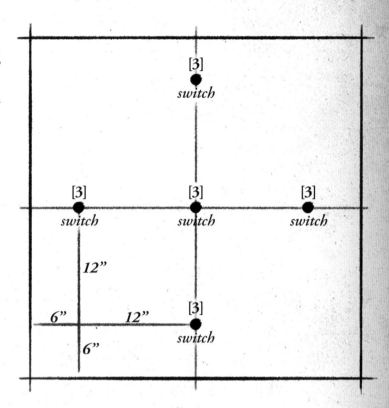

Pothill Market

The control of the Pothill market is crucial if our proceedings are to be unhindered! There should be no outsiders involved! This may be the greatest development of this era and I must report it to the High Committee personally! It just needs one more field test...

Before Deployment: Players alternate placing 4 Activated Objectives [3], Switch, 12" from table edges and 6" from the middle of the table. Place a single Activated Objective [3], Switch, in the middle of the table.

Enemy Models within 3" of an objective reduce the number of dice for Activating Objectives, one die per enemy Model.

Start of the game: Bid for the First Player as normal.

Deployment zones: Decided by the First Player.

Game length: The game lasts 3 turns. Last Chance.

Winning: A Player who controls 3 Objectives at the end of the last game turn is the winner.

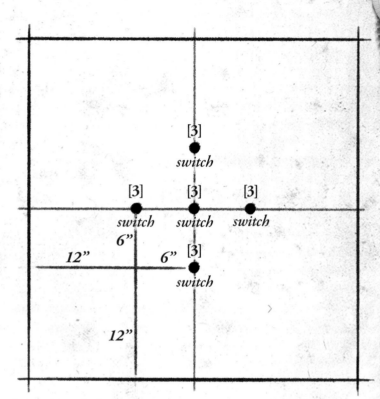

Stableton Cleaning

This whole place just needs some proper attention and it will shine. Just take care of these poor lost souls in that glorious if somewhat neglected house. And while you're at it, maybe send pneuma to Mayor about this pile of bricks, it will make a great museum! Are these gentlemen trying to install that hideous device in the centre of that square? That's unacceptable!

Before Deployment: Players alternate placing 4 Activated Objectives [3], Switch, 9" from adjacent table edges. Place a single Activated Objective [4], Switch, in the middle of the table.

Enemy Models within 3" of an objective reduce the number of dice for Activating Objectives, one die per enemy Model.

Start of the game: Bid for the First Player as normal.

Deployment zones: Decided by the First Player.

Game length: The game lasts 3 turns. Last Chance.

Winning: A Player who controls 3 Objectives at the end of any game turn is the winner.

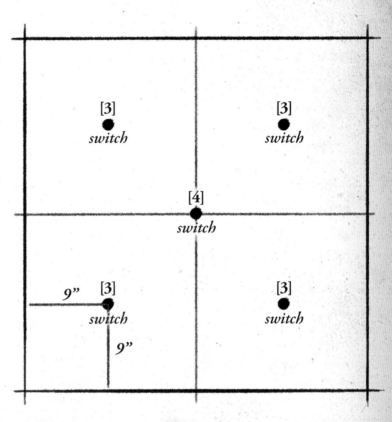

Showtime

Some people just cannot comprehend allusions. You have to show them exactly what you mean. Make them remember.

Hunt and be hunted! The only thing that matters in this scenario is killing enemy Heroes. It is vital to choose correct targets and protect your own high value Heroes.

Start of the game: Bid for the First Player as normal.

Deployment zones: Decided by the First Player.

Game length: The game lasts 3 turns.

Winning: A Player who killed enemy Heroes with the most Funds at the end of the 3rd turn is the winner.

This scenario was designed for tournament play to balance out one of the strategies to build the Club, which is the issue of a rich but weak Heroes in the company of many powerful Henchmen. This scenario gives an advantage to clubs that have decided to invest their funds in Heroes rather than Henchmen – the richer the Hero the more tempting a target. It may happen that one of the clubs will have to kill all enemy Heroes to offset the death of only one Hero.

Alternatively, you could design your own much more complex scenarios with Attacker and Defender clearly defined, following similar pattern to the "Free Henry" scenario presented below.

Free Henry! - An example of a complex scenario

They've taken Henry hostage! Fortunately, they've been thick enough to take him to their Headquarters. Now we know exactly where to strike!

Objectives: One of the Heroes from the Attacker's Club is being detained there in the middle of the Defender Club - the Defender chooses one of the Attacker's Hero Models to be the Prisoner and places it inside their Headquarters building.

The Prisoner cannot Activate until a friendly Model makes an "**Unbind**" **Quick Action** in BtB contact with the Prisoner Model.

The Prisoner is worth 5 Victory Points for the Defender if it is not freed (no "Unbind" Quick Action made) until the end of the game. If the Prisoner is freed and there is a Defender's Model in BtB with the Prisoner at the end of the game it is worth 3 Victory Points to the Defender instead. Otherwise it is worth 3 Victory Points to the Attacker.

Place at least 2 Activatable Objectives Switch[2] within 6" of the Headquater building. They are worth 2 Victory Points each at the end of the game if controlled.

Every enemy Henchman Model killed is worth 1 Victory Point. Every enemy Hero Model killed is worth 2 Victory Points.

Start of the game: Bid for the First Player as normal. The First Player is the Attacker.

Deployment zones: The Defender's Club is deployed completely inside a single building placed in the middle of the table - this is this Club's Headquarters.

The Attacker's Club is deployed anywhere on the table at least 6" from the Headquarters building.

Game length: The game lasts 3 turns.

Winning: The Player who scored the most Victory Points at the end of the 3rd turn is the winner.

Special Abilities

Armor Piercing [x]: When inflicting damage ignore x points of the Target Model's Armor.

Beginner's Luck: Once per game This Model may Re-roll all the dice it rolled in a single Test.

Fast Shot [x]: As a part of one Shoot Action this weapon may fire up to x times. Each subsequent shot is resolved at a cumulative -1G. Each shot in one Shoot Action may target a different Model but needs to be declared before any dice are rolled to do so. Calculate modifiers for each shot separately.

Fast Strike [x]: As a part of one Fight or Charge Action This Model may make up to x melee attacks. Each subsequent strike is resolved at a cumulative -1F. Each attack may target a different Model if able but needs to be declared before any dice are rolled to do so. A different Melee Reaction may be chosen against every attack.

Fiery Passion: This Model has Resistance to Fire [3].

Golem: This Model needs to start its Activation within a Control Range of a friendly Scientist and needs to stay in it during its whole Activation. If this Model by any reason starts its Activation out of the Control Range it must make Move Actions to get back into the Control Range of the closest friendly Scientist. If there are no friendly Scientists present on the battlefield this Model can't be Activated this turn. Golems have Fire Immunity. Golems are not Living Models.

Gruesome Damage: This model deals +2 damage, instead of +1, for each Critical Hit. This special rule only works in Melee unless it is conferred by a Ranged Weapon or it specifically states otherwise.

Hard to Kill: If This Model's Wounds are reduced to 0 and it had more than 1 Wound at the moment it suffered damage, it is reduced to 1 Wound instead.

Hypnotic Aura: Models may not choose a Fence Melee reaction when being attacked in Melee by This Model.

Immunity: Whenever This Model is targeted by an attack or effect it has Immunity against, the attack automatically misses and the effect is not applied.

Infiltrator: Instead of deploying This Model normally, place 3 markers anywhere outside the enemy's deployment zone, but no closer than 12" apart. At the start of the first game turn, roll a number of dice equal to This Model's Reflex. For each success the Opponent must choose one marker. You can now deploy This Model on any of the chosen markers. If there are no markers available for deployment, the enemy may place the Infiltrator anywhere outside of his deployment zone. It cannot be the first Model Activated on the turn it is deployed. It suffers the Move Penalty [1] to all its Actions on the turn it is deployed.

Instant: You may use this ability at the end of every Action, even if This Model had made another Action or Quick Action or is in base contact with an Enemy Model.

Living Model: Every Model that is not an Undead, a Golem or an Object is a Living Model unless noted otherwise.

Mindless Model: This Model has to be Activated before any friendly non-Mindless Models may be Activated. It may not attempt to Activate an Objective, but provides bonus for other Models attempting to do so as normal.

Move Penalty [x]: This Model suffers a penalty of x to it's Guns (to a minimum of 1) this Activation if it first made a Move Action, Charge Action or Moved as part of a Quick Action this Activation.

Natural Engineer [Action]: Once per game place a Golem Servant model in BtB with This Model. The Golem Servant has a *Golem* Ability and Armor [5]

Golem Servant		Actions	Move	Fight	Str	Guns	Reflex	Wounds
HENCHMAN Golem/30mm		2	4	3	4	2	2	4

Nexus [x], Magic Type: Models with a Magic Ability: [Magic Type] within 6" of a Model or Object with this rule gain +x to their Magic Ability.

Night Vision: This Model may trace LoS through Smoke Templates and ignores Low Visibility.

Protection [x]: Whenever This Model is targeted by an attack of a type it has Protection from it gains +x Reflex for the purpose of resolving of this attack.

Quick: This Model can make a Move and then perform the Action this rule applies to. This is not a Move Action (see Melee). Ranged Weapons with Quick rule suffer -1G Penalty if the model Moves and Shoots in the same Action. You cannot make more than one Quick Action per

Action. Always complete the movement before making the other activity.

Resistance [x]: Whenever This Model suffers damage of a type it is Resistant to, the Model gains +x unmodifiable Armor for purpose of resolving this damage.

Small Caliber: Double the Armor bonus when calculating damage from this weapon.

Swift: This Model may always use their Reflex instead of Fight when Parrying in Melee. It also automatically passes the test to Leave Melee.

Techniques of Sunnir Masters: This Model gains Protection [1] when targeted with enemy spells.

Template:

A Template is a 3" diameter circular area placed on the battlefield that remains in play until the end of turn.

The height of the Template is equal to its diameter unless the specific rules state otherwise.

A Model is Affected by a Template if it is within its area at any point during a game turn. The Effect of the Template is applied in the same Action the Model is first affected by it. A Model may only be Affected by each Template once during a game turn.

Examples of the most common Templates:

Fire Template: The area of this Template is Rough Ground. Effect: This Model suffers 2 Fire Damage, ignoring Armor (but not Fire Resistance).

Acid Template: Effect: This Model suffers 2 Acid Damage. If it has any Armor (but not Acid Resistance) it is reduced by 2 until end of turn.

Smoke Template: This Template blocks LoS through it. Models within it gain Cover [1].

Mist Template: This Template blocks LoS through it. Models within it gain Cover [1]. See Mist Walker and Mistaker.

Undead: This Model is not a Living Model. Cold Immunity, Fire Vulnerability.

Vulnerability: Double the damage This Model suffers from an attack of a type it is Vulnerable to.

ASH AND OAK

Ash and Oak Club

Ash and Oak Club

One day you realize that you have everything. High social standing, a sizable fortune, fame, education, a wide circle of acquaintances. You have achieved or inherited things for which ordinary people strive for whole generations. What does that leave you with? To look for ways to kill boredom. Concluding this lengthy digression, I'm betting another thousand that Miss Fearless won't manage to keep the golems from destroying the museum.

With great possibilities comes great responsibility. Noblesse oblige. These are not some empty platitudes. Even if the citizens of Lyonesse don't expect our help, we still have an obligation to protect them.

Would you then kindly put down that glass of bourbon, grab your shotgun, move your revered backside and follow me? We have a city to save.

I say, did you see the latest edition of "Lyonesse Crystalograph"? On the first page they only write about some new inventions and personalities from the world of science. My newest clothing design and the coverage of Baroness Nimblewist's charily ball got bumped to third and fourth pages. This is unacceptable! Tell a butler to heat up the boiler in the steamobile. We are off to inflict some headlines!

Just as   is the heart of the Alfheim Empire, the heart of the City of Cities is the historical Uldnesse district containing the Queen's palace, home of Parliament and the government. Everything here is as Alfish as possible: tea served at five, lukewarm beer in pubs, red pneuma booths, benches in the squares, carriages, tidy lawns and polite, disdain-filled emotional distance with which the locals look upon the rest of the world. The heart of Uldnesse is without a doubt the Ash and Oak club. At least that is what its members assume.

Club Activity

Ash and Oak is a world famous Lyonesse club for Extraordinary Ladies and Gentlemen. The club is renowned for its elegant, calm atmosphere, a well-stocked cellar and interesting lectures held in its chambers every month. All the members derive from the social elite. They do not have to be aristocrats or insanely rich industrialists – it is enough for them to be well-born, wealthy and famous.

Location and organisation

The seat of the Ash and Oak club is a vast, scenic building on Old Pyre Street, not one hundred meters from the church of St. Berenus, which conventionally designates the center of Lyonesse. The nearest Metropolitan Rail station (Central and Northern lines) – Kingchapel – is just a five-minute walk away. The current club president is Sir Zachary Fiercebatten. The ghastly old man keeps defending his position with the same sort of ferocity he employed during the Great War when repelling the undead attacks. Still, truth be told, the organization of everyday activities and actual control over the club's finances rests on the shoulders of countless armies of anonymous secretaries and butlers. Under Sir Zachary's leadership the Ash and Oak club strongly marks its presence within Lyonesse. After all, someone has to keep thwarting the criminal plans of the Triad of Lotus Dragon and temper the bloated egos of the eccentric inventors. There are various reasons why the club members keep engaging in increasingly violent scuffles with other organizations: an innate sense of justice, simple boredom or the need to satisfy one's ego. Unfortunately, the club is not monolithic – conservative aristocrats under the leadership of Lord Oakroot more and more openly compete with the "foreigners and upstarts" gathered around Mary Fearless.

Special Abilities

Noble: This is a keyword used to make other rules work with it. If a model has a Noble rule it is considered a Noble model and rules that require a Noble Model as a subject work with it.

	Actions	Move	Fight	Str	Guns	Reflex	Wounds
Captain Olafsson HERO Troll / 30mm	2	5	5	5	3	4	10

ABILITIES

Fiery Passion: This Model has Resistance to Fire [3].

Noble: This is a keyword used to make other rules work with it. If a model has a Noble rule it is considered a Noble model and rules that require a Noble Model as a subject work with it.

With me! [Quick Action]: Discard a card in this model's suit. Target friendly Bruiser or Butler Model in BtB with this model may be placed standing in BtB with this model after it finishes its Activation.

Look Out Milord!: While this model is on the battlefield friendly Noble models may transfer melee Damage they suffer to a friendly non-Toppled Bruiser within 6". The model the Damage is transferred to is placed in BtB with the transferring Noble model and is Toppled. If there is no room to place the model this ability cannot be used.

Fever: If This Model makes a Heroic Move friendly Models within 6" of This Model gain Fiery Passion.

Military Training: This model cannot be Toppled. When Jumping Heroically and non-Heroically this model gains +2M.

Breach!: When forcing a Locked Door open and attacking Objects in melee this model gains +3 Strength.

GADGETS

Troll's Temper: Melee Weapon. Fire damage. Sizzling Heat: Place a Fire Template centered over model hit.

"You ask if he's insanely brave, or just insane? During our defense of an outpost near Vergen, we saw a bundle of dynamite fall into our trench, its fuse lit and getting shorter by the second. Olafsson coolly picked up the charge, lit himself a cigarette with the spark, and casually threw the bomb back towards the enemy position. Nothing fancy, you say? First, he stopped to roll up that cigarette – did I mention that? Had to lend him some rolling paper. I've never been so scared in my life."

Captain Frederik Olafsson is definitely one of the bravest subjects of the Alfish Crown. He earned his first decorations during the War as a special forces soldier, taking part in the most risky operations of all the fronts. After the War, he worked with Her Majesty's secret intelligence service, protecting the citizens of Lyonesse all on his own. Awarded with the Silver Titania Moon as well as more than a dozen other royal decorations, he intends to collect them all – including the ones awarded posthumously.

ASH AND OAK

	Actions	Move	Fight	Str	Guns	Reflex	Wounds
Sir Lance Oakroot HERO Elf / 30mm	2	6	9	2	3	5	9

ABILITIES

Hypnotic Aura: Models may not Fence when being attacked in Melee by This Model.

Do not be silly!: Friendly Butlers gain the Hard to Kill rule.

Noble: This is a keyword used to make other rules work with it. If a model has a Noble rule it is considered a Noble model and rules that require a Noble Model as a subject work with it.

GADGETS

Sir Oakroot's top-hat: Once per game you may automatically Steal the Initiative. No cards are played.

D'Armanini Dress Suit*: +1R (included in the profile). This Model can never use Cover.

Creidnallen Rapier*: Melee Weapon. +3F (already included in the profile), Armor piercing [1].

„Jeeves, quit joking around! Stop bleeding at once and hand me the pistol."

„Please do not take my remark as overly boorish, but is this your first duel, sir? I could not help but notice that you were not able to execute a single effective attack in the last hour. But please, you needn't hurry, I can devote a bit more time to you. It is not until seven that I have my bridge appointment."

Sir Lance Oakroot, twelfth count of Drakespire is a descendant and heir to one of the oldest Alfish houses, a graduate of the University of Lyonesse, an unparalleled fencer and a merciless duelist. Sir Lance never parts with his hereditary blade made of creidnallen – enchanted elven silver. He also never shows up in public without the very newest, tailor-made attire and a fashionable top hat. It is said that even the decision to have his hand replaced with a golemic prosthesis had been dictated by fashion and fancy, rather than necessity. Like all counts of Drakespire, Master Lance treats gentlemen loftily, ladies gallantly, and servants instrumentally.

Lady Ellendeanne	Actions	Move	Fight	Str	Guns	Reflex	Wounds
HERO Elf / 30mm	2	6	3	2	2	4	9

3

ABILITIES

Hypnotic Aura: Models may not Fence when being attacked in Melee by This Model.

Noble: This is a keyword used to make other rules work with it. If a model has a Noble rule it is considered a Noble model and rules that require a Noble Model as a subject work with it.

GADGETS

Umbrella*: This Model gains +1F and +1R if targeted by a living Model from 12" or less.

Virtue: Ranged Weapon.

Name	S	0-8"	8-16"	16-24"	Notes
Virtue	4	+1	-1	-2	Quick, Hidden

Hidden: +1G for the first shot in each Activation

MAGIC

Magic Ability [4]: Spiritualism

	Type	Cost	Range	S	Notes
Mind Control	Magic Attack	1	18"	-	Mind Control

Mind Control: Target enemy Henchman makes one Action as if it was a friendly Model immediately after This Model's Activation.

	Type	Cost	Range	S	Notes
Inspire	Buff [2]	1	12"	-	Inspire

Inspire: If successful, the Target Model gains +1 Action in its next Activation.

„What do you think you're doing, young man?! Put down that death ray launcher this instant and stop aiming at Sir Zachary. If you want to have a shoot, kindly pick one of the golems that you dragged in with you."

„No self-respecting lady should leave the house without a solid umbrella. Personally, I prefer alchemically treated silk on a creidnallen frame. Protects brilliantly against sun, rain, saber strikes and small to medium caliber bullets."

Some say that for such a ludicrously rich aristocrat, Lady Petronella Ellendeanne spends too much time on the streets of Lyonesse, mingling with the commoners. Well, when one has hot-blooded Corioleans among their ancestors, one can allow herself any amount of eccentrics. The ability to call anyone to order with a single reproachful glance, be it a banker in Tintagel District, or a thug in the Bridgebank slums, comes in handy as well. Lady Elledeanne spends her spare time on fashion design and leading self-defense courses for the ladies.

Sir Zachary Fiercebatten	Actions	Move	Fight	Str	Guns	Reflex	Wounds
HERO Human / 30mm	2	3	2	2	7	2	9

ABILITIES

Old as the Hills: This model does not have the Beginner's Luck rule despite being a Human.

Noble: This is a keyword used to make other rules work with it. If a model has a Noble rule it is considered a Noble model and rules that require a Noble Model as a subject work with it.

GADGETS

Wheelchair: Cannot move in Rough Ground unless he uses Heroic Move. If Sir Fiercebatten starts his Activation in BtB with a friendly Butler or Bodyguard, he can make one free Move Action before he performs any other Actions.

Arcantric Monocle: This Model can draw LoS through Templates as if the target was in Cover [2].

Girardoni Windbüchse: Ranged Weapon.

	S	12-24"	24-36"	36"	Notes
Girandoni Windbüchse	3	+1	0	-1	Small Calibre

Small Calibre: Double the Armor bonus when calculating damage from this weapon.

"Faster Jeeves, faster! And stop panting so much, blast it! Honestly, when I was your age, I used to run cross country around the Ferret Forest all the while pushing a wheelchair with my paralyzed grandma, and I got second place! They gave the gold to granny…"

"Honestly, young man, you call that shooting? Back straighter, barrel higher, steady breaths! Honestly, in your age I used to blow off three zombie heads for every ten heartbeats. From three hundred yards! You wouldn't survive an hour on the front lines! I said steady your breath, blast it!!!"

No need to beat about the bush: Sir Zachary Fiercebatten, a decorated war hero, president of the Ash and Oak Club, the first human ever to be seated in the Alfheim House of Peers is a petty, half-deaf, despicable old man devoid of any positive emotions. He also has more than ninety years worth of experience in emerging unscathed from any and all dangerous situations, shouting out orders and mentally abusing the youth. Sir Zachary does not even think about retirement, and the only sort of entertainment he accepts is attending the funerals of his political opponents.

Zachary Fiercebatten III

HERO
Human / 30mm

Actions	Move	Fight	Str	Guns	Reflex	Wounds
2	5	2	3	2	3	11

FUNDS 2

ABILITIES

Beginner's Luck: Once per game This Model may Reroll all the dice it rolled in a single Test.

Noble: This is a keyword used to make other rules work with it. If a model has a Noble rule it is considered a Noble model and rules that require a Noble Model as a subject work with it.

"Master" Gunner: This Model can re-roll any dice on G or F tests as long as a friendly Singh also has LoS to the target.

Release the Hounds! [Quick Action]: Once per game. Place 2 Hounds in BtB with Zachary. The next Activated Models have to be the Hounds, afterwards the Initiative is resolved as normal.

GADGETS

Safari apparel: Armor [1]

.577 Nitro Express Rifle: Ranged Weapon.

	S	0-12"	12-24"	Notes
.577 Nitro Express	10	+1	-1	Move Penalty[1]

"See, Abihnav? Watch and learn. This is how you shoot. Because you, as usual, missed the target and shot Sir Lance's top hat off. You have to practice more, Abihnav. Practice makes perfect."

"Tear him to shreds! Get him! Get him, you dumb dogs... Kindly forgive the fawning, sir, they still haven't finished their training."

Zachary Fiercebatten III is a grandson of the well-known and decorated war veteran Sir Zachary Fiercebatten. Unlike his grandfather, Zach is slightly less… capable. This does not stop him from enjoying a life of game hunting and boasting. His family's great wealth allows him to run lavish "before hunting expedition" and "after hunting expedition" parties, which can drag on up to a fortnight and take place in up to a dozen different family estates. He is always sure to bring the largest and newest gun and only the best beverages to a hunt. Zach loves his Basset dogs and believes them to be the greatest and bravest hunting hounds, with tracking abilities second to none. Nobody has the nerve to tell him otherwise.

Hound

HENCHMAN
Hound / 30mm

Actions	Move	Fight	Str	Guns	Reflex	Wounds
1	9	2	3	0	4	2

n/a COST

ABILITIES

Hunting Pack: Both of the Zachary's hounds must remain within 6" of one another, and are Activated at the same time.

Find the Prey!: When the Hound is attacking in close combat, the enemy Model cannot Fence.

Mary Fearless

HERO
Human / 30mm

Actions	Move	Fight	Str	Guns	Reflex	Wounds
2	5	3	3	4	4	9

2 FUNDS

ABILITIES

Beginner's Luck: Once per game this Model may Re-roll all the dice it rolled in a single test.

Noble: This is a keyword used to make other rules work with it. If a model has a Noble rule it is considered a Noble model and rules that require a Noble Model as a subject work with it.

Rencontre: When being shot at, instead of rolling a number of dice equal to R, Mary rolls a number of dice equal to G. If she rolls more successes than the Shooting Model, calculate the damage as if Mary were the Shooting Model, and the Shooting Model were the Target Model.

GADGETS

Colt Navy: Ranged Weapon.

Name	S	0-8"	8-16"	16-24"	Notes
Colt Navy	4	+1	-1	-2	Quick, Fast Shot [2]

"My dear sir, my name is Mary Fearless. I was a sheriff in Undeadwood, the sole survivor of the Nope Corral shootout, and I can put down a charging werebison with a single shot. Do you think some Pothill thug would scare me?"

"Go ahead. Reach for the gun and make my day."

Mary Fearless was born in Vinlandian Alfheim as Mary Winterbough III. During the uprising in the colonies she took the rebels' side and avoided death penalty only through the intercession of certain well-born relatives. At the moment, if she is not hunting bandits and bison on the western territory prairies, she spends her time in the clubs and theatres of Lyonesse – hiding under an assumed name, right under the nose of Alven Yard. She is the first woman in Alfheim who – insulted – challenged a man to a duel. Needless to say, she won.

Ash and Oak
HENCHMEN

Butler	Actions	Move	Fight	Str	Guns	Reflex	Wounds
HENCHMAN Human / 30mm	2	5	2	3	2	3	9

COST 1

ABILITIES

Helping Hand: Friendly Heroes within 6" may discard a card of ANY suit to use Heroic Move.

What do I pay you for!: If a friendly Noble Model loses any number of W from shooting, a friendly non-Toppled Butler within 6" may lose that many W instead. This Butler is placed in the line of fire and in BtB with the Noble Model and is Toppled.

GADGETS

Pistol: Ranged Weapon.

	S	0-8"	8-16"	16-24"	Notes
Pistol	4	+1	-1	-2	Quick

"Your gun and scented handkerchief, Sir. Let me also mention that we have arranged a tea break with Doctor Doom's insane assistants. It starts in a quarter of an hour, Sir. I would be grateful if you take it into consideration while planning your combat maneuvers."

The spiteful claim that an aristocrat is worth as much as their best butler. There is quite a bit of truth in it. Well trained butlers are indispensable both at home and on the battlefield. A pistol handed at the right moment, an arm to lean on, or a faithful servant to take the bullet intended for his master can easily turn the tide of battle. Besides, only barbarians go to battle without someone who can properly brew and serve tea.

Bruiser	Actions	Move	Fight	Str	Guns	Reflex	Wounds
HENCHMAN Ogre / 30mm	2	5	4	7	2	2	15

2 COST

ABILITIES

Hard to Kill: If this Model's Wounds are reduced to 0 and it had more than 1 Wound at the moment it suffered damage, it is reduced to 1 Wound instead.

GADGETS

Bodyguard livery: Armor [1]

"Is this golem bothering you, Miss? I thought so. (Sound of crushed metal)."

Ogre bruisers are always in fashion. Competent, abnormally strong, insanely loyal, extremely tough to kill, and furthermore they look absolutely to die for in well-cut liveries. Basically they have but one, tiny flaw – an unfortunate tendency to fall in love with the female clients. It has to be noted that ogres are exceedingly competent in that field as well.

ASH AND OAK

Singh	Actions	Move	Fight	Str	Guns	Reflex	Wounds
HENCHMAN Orc / 30mm	2	5/	3	3	4	4	8

COST 2

ABILITIES

Infiltrator: Instead of deploying the Model normally, place 3 markers anywhere outside the enemy's deployment zone and no closer than 12" apart. At the start of the first game turn, roll a number of dice equal to this Model's Reflex. For each success the enemy must choose one marker this Model can be deployed on. If there are no markers available for deployment, the enemy may place the Infiltrator anywhere outside of his deployment zone. It cannot be the first Model Activated on the turn it is deployed. It suffers the **Move Penalty [1]** to all its Actions on the turn it is deployed.

GADGETS

Singh Uniform: Armor [1]

Hunting Rifle: Ranged Weapon.

	S	0-8"	8-16"	16-24"	Notes
Hunting Rifle	6	0	-1	-2	Move Penalty [1]

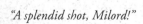

"A splendid shot, Milord!"

The quiet and mysterious Dekanian used to be an aide of Sir Zachary Fiercebatten. Today, with equal dedication and unrelenting patience, he takes care of Sir Zachary's grandson. It is said that apart from his excellent marksmanship, he has also learned the secrets of the Dekanian yogis. Reportedly, he is able to sleep on nails, fast for whole months, move soundlessly, bear any and all hardships, and stay completely still on a designated post for hours on end. The best proof of Singh being a genuine enlightened yogi is his unshakable serenity when dealing with young Master Zachary's buffoonery.

Sir Lance Oakroot

Lady Petronella
Ellendeanne

Mary Fearless

Singh

Butler

Butler

Sir Zachary Fiercebatten

Ogre Bruiser

Ogre Bruiser

Zachary Fiercebatten III

Lady Dorothy Quimby

INVENTORS

Inventors

Inventors Club

They laughed at me! They called me mad! They said that transferring such complicated machinery into the Astral is impossible, reckless and dangerous!

We'll see who's laughing when an army of my golems materializes right in the center of Abbot's Gardens!!! Reckless and dangerous, please...

The energy beam passes through a complex system of crystal lenses and prisms, and then radiates in a direction chosen by the operator. It is a working solution to the wireless energy transfer problem. The power of a thousand steam boilers focused in one tiny point the size of a pinhead. Unfortunately, the beam has a troubling tendency of incinerating any objects in its path. I think I'll shelve this project, as I can't think of any practical application for this contraption.

If you asked me what the highest value is, I would answer: Progress. It is our responsibility to push the boundaries of science in every field, at every moment, and by any means necessary. So, when I give you the signal with this flag, put on your headphones and push that red button over there.

During the first World Exhibition in Orseaux many a famous inventor stumbled upon something previously inconceivable – rivals, whose projects could not be scornfully dismissed. A year later the Inventors Club has been established. The official goal of the organization is to expand the boundaries of science, but in reality, the idea is to finally determine who among the members is endowed with the greatest of intellects.

Club activity

Any scientist who independently designed and constructed a brand new, unique invention can become a club member. Of course, they still have to present it before the club presidium and survive the inevitable onslaught of negative comments. Since the prevalent inventions are usually golems or new types of weapons and powered armor, and the ones presenting tend not to respond well to criticism, the hearings of the candidates are often... interesting. The percentage of fatal accidents is relatively low, though, and the club is slowly growing.

Location and organisation

The elite organization of megalomaniacal technomages is based in Lyonesse, and that is where the club members arrange presentations of most of their inventions. The establishment's main headquarters is housed in Myrkwood Park of the Windbog district – inside the mansion of Winston Falconwing, Esq. – an arrogant half-elf and club president. While Sir Winston disappeared while testing an astral teleportation machine a few months ago, the rest of the scientists don't seem to mind, as they readily enjoy the abundant wine cellar and cozy rooms of the president's house.

As is easy to deduce, the Inventors Club functions in a delightfully uncoordinated manner. Every scientist has their own idea for promoting science and publicly presenting the latest inventions. Unfortunately, the tests, unsanctioned by the city officials, often get out of control and cause constant clashes with the self-proclaimed guardians of Lyonesse from the Ash and Oak Club. No less bothersome are the incessant attempts by the Triad of Lotus Dragon, which would happily put its paws on some of the more dangerous inventions. As if that was not enough, Lord Falconwing's prolonged absence drags on, and sooner or later the scientists will be forced to elect a new president. That never occurs without casualties.

Special Abilities

Scientist: This model has the ablity to control friendly Golems within a 12" Control Range.

Golem: This Model needs to start its Activation within a Control Range of a friendly Scientist and needs to stay in it during its whole Activation. If this Model by any reason starts its Activation out of the Control Range it must make Move Actions to get back into the Control Range of the closest friendly Scientist. If there are no friendly Scientists present on the battlefield this Model can't be Activated this turn. Golems have Fire Immunity. Golems are not Living Models.

Onuphrius Myshkin	Actions	Move	Fight	Str	Guns	Reflex	Wounds
HERO Gnome / 30mm	2	5	3	3	3	3	9

3 FUNDS

ABILITIES

Scientist: This model has the ablity to control friendly Golems within a 12" Control Range.

Forced Evolutionist: At the start of the First Turn place one friendly Onuphrius's Mice Model in BtB with This Model.

GADGETS

Apron: Armor [1]

"You're saying that I don't adhere to the scientific method? Balderdash! I am improving upon it! My underachieving colleagues keep experimenting on white mice – mindless rodents that don't even grasp the basic concept of science. I use golemic mice, which are programmed to understand the purpose of the experiment and behave accordingly. Science is too serious a matter to leave anything to chance."

This rather eccentric gnome of Slavic origins is known for his peculiar fixation on rodents. Perhaps, as a child, he was enthralled by the Slavic fairy tale about certain mice that ate the corpse of a dragoness, thus gaining superpowers? It is hard to say. Myshkin does not mention his past, completely focusing on his experiments and getting closer to his dream, which involves recognition, fame, fortune, and lots and lots of cheese.

MAGIC

Magic Ability [3]: Technomagic.

	Type	Cost	Range	S	Notes
Direct Control	Buff [2]	x	self	-	Direct Control

Direct Control: One Golem model in BtB with This Model or a friendly Onuphrius's Mice Model gains +xM, +xF. Make an Action with this Golem after This Model finishes its Activation.

	Type	Cost	Range	S	Notes
So Mice	Buff [1]	0	18"	-	So Mice

So Mice: Make an Action with a friendly Onuphrius's Mice model within range after This Model finished its Activation. For this Action the Onuphrius's Mice count as a Hero model of the same suit as This Model.

If there is no friendly Onuphrius's Mice Model on the battlefield, place one friendly Onuphrius's Mice Model in BtB with This Model.

Onuphrius's Mice	Actions	Move	Fight	Str	Guns	Reflex	Wounds
HENCHMAN Mice/ 30mm	1	7	1	1	1	5	2

n/a COST

ABILITIES

Shouldermice: If a friendly model starts its Move action in BtB with This Model, during the friendly model's Activation This Model may be moved with it by placing it in BtB with the moving model at the end of its Action.

Squeek: This model counts as a friendly Scientist for friendly Golem models within 6".

Vulnerability [Cat]: This Model is Vulnerable to Cats.

INVENTORS

Thorvald Nielsgaard

HERO
Human / 30mm

Actions	Move	Fight	Str	Guns	Reflex	Wounds
2	5	4	7	3	3	11

2 FUNDS

ABILITIES

Scientist: This model has the ablity to control friendly Golems within a 12" Control Range.

Beginner's Luck: Once per game This Model may Reroll all the dice it rolled in a single Test.

GADGETS

Arcantric Arm*: Melee Weapon. +4 Strength (included in the profile).

Reflector Field: Armor [3] against Shooting Attacks.

MAGIC

Magic Ability [4]: Technomagic

	Type	Cost	Range	S	Notes
Lightning	Projectile	0	12"	3	Galvanic

	Type	Cost	Range	Notes
Shimmer Field	Aura [2]	1	6"	Shield

	Type	Cost	Range	Notes
Arcantric Field	Aura [2]	2	6"	Shield, Armor [2]

Shield: Once cast the Field has 10 Wounds and this particular spell cannot be cast by This Model again until the corresponding Field reaches 0 Wounds. Whenever a magical or non-magical Ranged Attack hits a Model within this spell's range the damage is transferred to the Field the Player who controls This Model chooses after adding critical hits but before applying Armor of the targeted Model. Arcantric Field applies Armor [2] to the damage it takes. If the Field reaches 0 wounds the spell expires. Targeted Model suffers the excess damage as if it was a new attack hitting it once the Field expires.

INVENTORS

"The operation principle of the Spiritechnic Missile Deflector is surprisingly simple. I use a complicated system of runic gears, which unleash a spell, which sets the shielded objects into astral vibrations. That is to say, the objects are very quickly being transported between the physical reality and the spirit realm. Meanwhile, all accelerated objects are put into an inverse vibration. As a result, when the bullet is in our world, the shielded person is in the Astral, and the other way around. It all happens very fast, hence the faint shimmer. Dangerous? Why would it be dangerous?"

"Let me present another curious fact. A press of a button and... (deafening noise). I do hope you weren't all that attached to that arbor, my lady."

A young, ambitious scientist from Jøtunheim, exploring hazardous issues from within the bounds of technomagic and spiritism. His uncompromising approach to research made him a lot of enemies, and prompted him to leave the country in a hurry. Mr Nielsgaard currently resides in Lyonesse, where he continues his research under the wing of the Inventors Club. On further acquaintance he turns out to be as nice as he is insane – and one has to admit him to be exceedingly nice.

	Actions	Move	Fight	Str	Guns	Reflex	Wounds
Thomas Rocketheart Jr. HERO Dwarf / 30mm	2	4	3	4	4	2	13

ABILITIES

Scientist: This model has the ablity to control friendly Golems within a 12" Control Range.

Heavy Smoker [Quick Action]: Place a Smoke Template in BtB with this Model.

Night Vision: This Model may trace LoS through Smoke Templates and ignores Low Visibility.

GADGETS

Magneton Boots: This Model may perform Heroic Move and Heroic Recovery without discarding a card. Effects that reduce movement have no effect on this Model regardless of their kind. If a friendly Golem with a larger base starts his Move Action in BtB with this Model, during the Golem's Activation this Model may be moved with by placing it in BtB with the moving Golem at the end of it's Action.

Scorcher: Ranged Weapon.

	S	0-8"	8-16"	Notes
Scorcher	5	+1	-1	**Fire,** Fire Template

Fire Template: When using this weapon choose a target in range and place the 3" Fire Template completely over it. Make a Ranged Attack against each Model touched by the Template then leave it on the battlefield. Remove this Template at the end of turn.

"I've been signing contracts and negotiating with the workers for half a day, and then it turned out that the difference engine went haywire. I had to make the decision to demolish the entire west wing of the factory. On the other hand, I was able to get some exercise and test out the new equipment. Plus, there's nothing like lighting a good cigar off a giant steel golem's burning wreckage after a hard day's work..."

"Dunn-duh-duh-DUNNN-DUNN, Dunn-duh-duh-DUNNN-DUNN! (Music from the gramophone gets gradually replaced with explosion noises) I love the smell of phlogiston in the morning!"

Thomas Rockheart Jr is the president of Rokheart & Rockheart Automatonics, which, after the recent merger with Wotanian Steinfaust Kohl und Eisen, became one of the biggest corporations onthe islands. The ambitious dwarf practically never leaves the design office in Blackstone, where he personally tests all the prototypes getting prepared for production. Mr Rockheart smokes like a chimney, firmly believes in his own indestructibility, and has probably never even heard of health and safety protocols.

Ingrid Rangvaldottir

HERO
Troll / 30mm

Actions	Move	Fight	Str	Guns	Reflex	Wounds
2	5	3	5	4	4	10

n/a FUNDS

ABILITIES

Fiery Passion: Resistance to Fire [3].

Miraculous Mirrors: Ingrid always comes equipped with 3 Mirror Servants.

Scientist: This model has the ablity to control friendly Golems within a 12" Control Range.

GADGETS

Sun Spear: Ranged Weapon.

	S	∞"	Notes
Sun Spear	4	0	Fire, *Beam*

Beam: Beam is special kind of linear Template. When shooting weapon with this rule trace a straight line between this Model and the chosen point in its LoS and continue this in a straight line beyond this point until it no longer is in LoS or reaches the edge of the battlefield. This Model may target all Models in LoS and touched by the Beam Template.

Indeed, I do believe that a golem with a mirror is always useful to a lady on the battlefield. I'm not only taking about quick hair or makeup adjustments – a mirror also allows one to safely check if something unpleasant isn't lurking behind the corner. We attain the greatest utility, though, when we put several mirrors in various strategic points in the area. For example, let's take that orkish assassin hiding behind that steamobile, thinking nobody's seen him..."

"How does my Sun Spear work? I'll explain it as simply as possible. As a child, have you ever tried looking at ants on a sunny day through a magnifying glass?"

Ingrid Rangvaldottir earned the title of engineer at the Heimburg Technical University at the age of seventeen, a year later got the Master's degree in thaumology at the Montefalco University, and before turning twenty, she got her Ph.D. at the Feirn University. Her paper on unconventional ways of utilizing solar power earned her popular acclaim. Currently, Doctor Rangvaldottir teaches at the Lyonesse University, publishes in major scientific journals and collects notes for her postdoctoral degree.Taking into account Ingrid's scientific achievements and temperament, no one dares to comment on her fondness for high lace boots, daring low-cut corsets and gaudy jewelry.

Mirror Servant

HENCHMAN
Golem / 30mm

Actions	Move	Fight	Str	Guns	Reflex	Wounds
1	7	1	1	0	4	2

n/a LOST

ABILITIES

Golem: This Model needs to start its Activation within a Control Range of a friendly Scientist and needs to stay in it during its whole Activation. If this Model by any reason starts its Activation out of the Control Range it must make Move Actions to get back into the Control Range of the closest friendly Scientist. If there are no friendly Scientists present on the battlefield this Model can't be Activated this turn. Golems have Fire Immunity. Golems are not Living Models.

Armor [3]

One Purpose: All the friendly Mirror Servants Activate in the same Activation.

Mirror: Ingrid may elect to use Mirror Servants to extend her LoS. You may pick any targets that are in LoS of a Mirror Servant that has LoS to Ingrid. You may also trace Ingrid's LoS between several Servants and the target.

Redirect: When Sun Spear Beam Template passes through Mirror Servant in Ingrid's LoS, this Mirror Servant may change the direction of the Beam Template. End Sun Spear's Beam Template in base contact with this Mirror Servant. Then continue it by starting it again from the Mirror Servant's base using Beam rule. Each Mirror Servant may reflect the shot only once by shot. Don't resolve shooting attack against Mirror Servant that redirected the Beam Template that way.

INVENTORS

Alice Tinkerly

HERO
Human / 30mm

Actions	Move	Fight	Str	Guns	Reflex	Wounds
2	5	3	6	3	3	9

3 FUNDS

ABILITIES

Scientist: This model has the ablity to control friendly Golems within a 12" Control Range.

Beginner's Luck: Once per game This Model may Re-roll all the dice it rolled in a single test.

Engineer: [Quick Action] Once per Activation This Model may use one of the following effects on a friendly Golem in BtB:

• **Power Flux:** Until the end of turn the Golem icreases its Armor by 2

• **Overcharge:** Until the end of turn the Golem gains +2 M and +2 S

• **Repair:** The Golem is immediately restored to its full Wounds

GADGETS

Huge Wrench*: Melee Weapon, +2 S (*: included in the profile)

MAGIC

Magic Ability [3]: Technomagic

	Type	Cost	Range	Notes
Command	Buff [1]	1	12"	Command

Command: Choose a friendly Golem within range. The Golem may perform one Action as a part of an extra Activation after This Model ends its Activation, then the spell expires.

"So you're saying, Mr Vendetta, that the Cleaner golem, which you've turned in for maintenance, isn't working properly and you want to file a complaint? So it's not supposed to wipe dust and polish furniture? Just a moment, let me check my notes. Oh yes, I'd been repairing grandma Sweetbagle's golemic butler at that time. I must've accidentally mixed up the runic plates... Right! That would explain that shootout in the Clairvale nursing home they wrote about in the papers today. I like golems."

"They're much more logical and predictable than people. Do you know that a standard theater golem recognizes over ten thousand words? That's several times more than your average Lyonesse cabby."

Not much is known about Alice Tinkerly's past. One day she just appeared in the workshops of Windbog, casually fine-tuned a couple of steamobiles and straightaway became the favorite assistant of all the mechanics. When she built a functional golem out of parts found in the junkyard, the foremen joined forces in writing a letter of recommendation and sent Alice for a meeting to the Inventors Club. A couple of humiliated scientists later, miss Tinkerly became the youngest club member. Currently, she spends most of her time on the racetracks in Windbog testing out new models of golems. Almost no one believes the rumors of Alice being raised by gremlins. It would explain her total lack of social skills, though.

Snorri Rottstein	Actions	Move	Fight	Str	Guns	Reflex	Wounds
HERO Gnome/ 40mm	3	5	2	6	3	4	12

ABILITIES

Scientist: This model has the ablity to control friendly Golems within a 12" Control Range.

Natural Engineer: Action, once per game. Place a **Golem Servant** Model (see page 55) in BtB wih This Model.

GADGETS

Golemic Flea: Base size 40mm

Bash: Models hit by This Model in Melee are Toppled.

Flea Jump: This Model may perform Heroic Move without discarding a card.

Ride: [Quick Action] Once per Activation. If This Model starts its Action in BtB with a friendly Model mounted on a 30mm base, it may be placed in BtB with This Model again after This Model Moves. This may cause the placed Model to enter or leave Melee.

MAGIC

Magic Ability [4]: Technomagic

	Type	Cost	Range	Notes
Galvanic Blast	Magic Attack	1	6"	**Blast, Topple.**

Blast: This spell affects all enemy Models in range. Test once for Magic Ability and compare it to Reflex tests of all enemy Models in range.

Topple: Models hit are Toppled.

"I have heard that Lord Oakroot likes to brag about his brand new sport steamobile being able to outstrip any other vehicle in Lyonesse. I'm willing to accept this dare and prove the superiority of my Golemic Flea. Provided, of course, that I get to pick the route. Gentlemen, a toast to a fair competition!"

"Miss shouldn't touch! I've installed a couple of anti-vandal security measures. Miss wouldn't want to receive a sudden nasty mana shock, would she? A beautiful vehicle, isn't it? I have been watching a flea circus in Abbot's Gardens once, and that's when the project originated. And since we're already taking about entertainment, does miss have any plans for the afternoon? I know a lovely cafe in Tinkerton... Please allow me to introduce myself. My name is Snorri Rottstein and today my flea is at your disposal."

It is said that the eccentric inventor of the Golemic Flea spends as much time in his workshop in Svart Thule as in the cafés and cabinets of curiosities of Abbot's Gardens. His unconventional approach to life also manifests itself in his projects, of which every one is as brilliant as it is grotesque. Snorri Rottstein is known for his fondness for good liquor, operetta music and the company of women. As of now, he remains unmarried.

Lab Assistant	Actions	Move	Fight	Str	Guns	Reflex	Wounds
HENCHMAN Human / 30mm	2	5	2	3	2	3	9

COST 1

GADGETS

Lab Flask: Ranged Weapon.

	S	8"	Notes
Lab Flask	0	+1	Quick, *Unintentional result*

Unintentional result: When the target is hit with the Lab Flask roll a D6 and refer to the following chart:

1 – Smoke: Center a 3" Smoke Template on the target. Remove it at the end of the turn.

2 – Empty: The target suffers a S 3 hit.

3 – Acid: The target's Armor is reduced by 4 until the end of the game. If the target has no Armor it suffers a S 4 hit.

4 – Glue: The Model hit is Toppled

5 – Mercury Fumes: Center a 3" Smoke Template on the target. Each living Model starting its Activation within or moving through the Template suffers 2 W. Remove the Template at the end of the turn.

6 – Nitroglycerine: Center a 3" Smoke Template on the target. The target suffers a S 6 hit, all Models touching the Template are Toppled. Remove the Template at the end of the turn.

"I brought the reagents you asked for, sir. Yes, they're definitely the right ones. The ones from the third shelf, second compartment. Or was it second shelf, third compartment? Well, never mind... Oh! The liquid in the test tube changed color to red and keeps smoking something fierce. Is that good, professor? Profes... (sound of an explosion)."

A good assistant is a treasure. He will clean the test tubes, wipe off the acid stains, feed the hungry monstrosity in the basement, oil the golem, help out in testing out the mana-guided missiles, draft up a boring article for the upcoming conference, hold the lightning rod during a thunderstorm... All eccentric scientists know that one should value their assistants. They leave so fast.

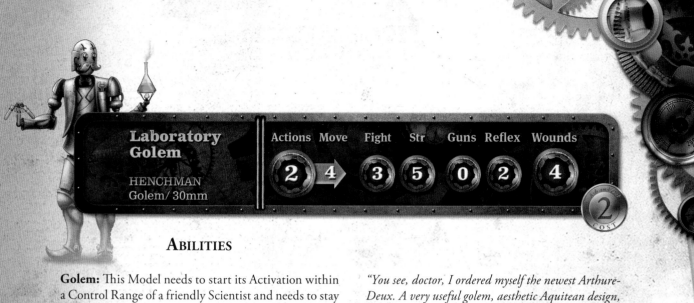

Laboratory Golem

HENCHMAN
Golem / 30mm

Actions	Move	Fight	Str	Guns	Reflex	Wounds
2	4	3	5	0	2	4

COST 2

Abilities

Golem: This Model needs to start its Activation within a Control Range of a friendly Scientist and needs to stay in it during its whole Activation. If this Model by any reason starts its Activation out of the Control Range it must make Move Actions to get back into the Control Range of the closest friendly Scientist. If there are no friendly Scientists present on the battlefield this Model can't be Activated this turn. Golems have Fire Immunity. Golems are not Living Models.

Armor [7]

"You see, doctor, I ordered myself the newest Arthure-Deux. A very useful golem, aesthetic Aquitean design, choice of three modes: cleaning, lab work and retreat. It doesn't work very well independently, but we wouldn't want unsupervised machines to perform experiments in our laboratories, would we? Ha ha, what an absurd thought... "

There are tasks that even the most desperate and loyal of assistants will not perform. In these kinds of situations, a reasonable scientist turns to laboratory golems. They are slow and not overly bright, but they remain functional even in extreme circumstances, and perform their tasks with the utmost literalism. In addition, they turned out to have quite a lot of applications on the battlefield. That is more than one can expect from an average live assistant.

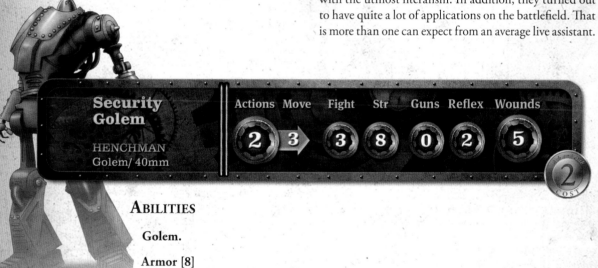

Security Golem

HENCHMAN
Golem / 40mm

Actions	Move	Fight	Str	Guns	Reflex	Wounds
2	3	3	8	0	2	5

COST 2

Abilities

Golem.

Armor [8]

Trample [Action]: This Model may make a Melee Attack against each Enemy Model within 1". To use this special ability This Model has to be in BtB with at least one Enemy Model. Roll separately against each Model. Models may not Fence if not in BtB with the Attacking Model.

Juggernaut: This Model ignores Rough Ground when moving. Additionally, it may Move through Impassable Ground but cannot end Move inside it.

See that beauty, madam? I built it based on the patterns of some battle golem back from the times of the War. I bought the construction plans in an antique shop in Heimburg. They were a bit nibbled on by mice and stained with some dark liquid, but it looks like I recreated all of the control runes correctly. It's better not to speak Wotanian in front of it, though, you could trigger some old algorithm."

The technomages do not know the meaning of fair competition. Sabotage, project theft and industrial espionage are the order of the day. No wonder more and more scientists invest in heavy and armored security machines. As they say, better safe than sorry. As a result, a giant steam golem entering through a wall becomes an increasingly common final argument during scientific debates.

INVENTORS

Clockwork Servant	Actions	Move	Fight	Str	Guns	Reflex	Wounds
HENCHMAN Golem/ 30mm	1	7	1	1	0	4	2

COST 1

ABILITIES

Golem: This Model needs to start its Activation within a Control Range of a friendly Scientist and needs to stay in it during its whole Activation. If this Model by any reason starts its Activation out of the Control Range it must make Move Actions to get back into the Control Range of the closest friendly Scientist. If there are no friendly Scientists present on the battlefield this Model can't be Activated this turn. Golems have Fire Immunity. Golems are not Living Models.

Armor [4]

Specialisation: Choose one role for each Clockwork Servant before deployment for the duration of the game: (The roles are defined by the actual Model you're using):

Oiler: [Quick Action] Friendly Golem in BtB gains +1M and +1F until end of turn.

Tinker: As long as This Model is in play, replace any friendly Golems with Wreck marker when they are reduced to 0 Wounds. [Quick Action] Friendly Golem in BtB recovers 1W. [Quick Action] Friendly Hero within 6" discards a card in his or her suit: Replace a Wreck Marker in BtB with the same type of Golem it was before at 1W remaining.

Booster: Whenever a friendly Hero discards a card during their Activation or a spell is cast within 12", This Model stores 1 charge. Friendly Golems within 6" may use a charge prior to making a dice roll to gain: This Model may re-roll any number of the dice it rolled this test.

"Tired of pungent smoke and clouds of steam hanging in the air? Your golem's mana batteries discharged for the umpteenth time? Your assistant indisposed again? The solution: Clockwork Servant Automatons - innovatory constructs combining the ingenious ideas of Renaissance masters with the precision of Westrian watchmakers. Made from cutting-edge materials, sold in packs of three along with a spare set of springs. Order today! When brute force fails, a reasonable scientist looks for an alternative solution."

Clockwork mechanism-powered servant automatons are the favorite kind of support of the technomages, who value responsiveness and flexibility. The little automatons can serve as an early warning system, scouts, or portable magic energy amplifiers. It is best to wind them up in the evening, just before going to bed. They work great as alarm clocks, too.

Ingrid Rangvaldottir and Golems

Lab Assistant

Alice Tinkerly

Thorvald Nielsgaard

Thomas Rockheart Jr

Lab Golem

Lab Golem

Galvanizer

Snorri Rottstein

Security Golem

Triad of Lotus Dragon

Triad of Lotus Dragon

The Dragon Emperor is asleep in the distant Forbidden City, but it does not make us defenseless. Among the fog and lotus smoke hides our own dragon, who has hundreds of eyes and hundreds of legs and who protects us. The long noses do not believe its existence, but they have never understood anything. The Alfish believe that they have humiliated our empire, that they have brought it to its knees. They think they can sail their battleships into our harbors, open their trading posts and ship out our treasures for next to nothing. We shall endure it with humility, while living in the heart of their kingdom, studying their way of life and learning the secrets of their technology. And when we are ready, we will rise up and bring them to their knees. Take a look at Pothill. Compared to the rest of Lyonesse, it is a dump – overcrowded slums full of desperate immigrants. Such life is not enough for me. I want my children to go to the best schools, drive luxurious steamobiles and drink tea with milk in exclusive clubs. I shall fulfill this dream, no matter how many people will have to pay for it. I want you to keep this in mind whilst considering my offer. No one is sure whether the Triad of Lotus Dragon came to Alfheim from the Dragon Empire or was conceived within the alleys and dens of Shang-Town. One thing is for sure – when the Lyonesse constables acknowledged the illegal lotus trade to be a serious problem, and when they began to venture into the depths of Pothill, they found the sophisticated criminals tattooed with the sign of the lotus dragon already there. Nothing seems to suggest them planning to leave Lyonesse anytime in the future.

Club activity

Officially, what the Triad of Lotus Dragon does is teach martial arts, look out for immigrants from the Dragon Empire and promote Shangese culture. Unofficially, it also deals in extortion, prostitution, art smuggling, industrial espionage and black lotus trade. Pothill residents see no problem with that. The rest of Lyonesse has a different opinion, however.

Location and organisation

No one knows the location of the Triad of Lotus Dragon's main headquarters. Their members always appear where they are most needed – or most feared. Orkish gentlemen can sometimes be seen conversing over a mahjong board and a cup of tea. Supposedly Xen Jidao and Mr Cheng always meet up during the performances of the Shang In National Opera. These might be just rumors, however. Few realize that a fierce struggle for power is taking place within the organization. Xen Jidao and his loyal traditionalists think that the organization ought to work in exactly the same way as the triads in the old country, focusing on lotus trade, martial arts and the "protection" of the merchants. This stands in opposition to the innovative vision of Mr Cheng. Inspired by other gangs, he continues to expand the organization's activity in the field of prostitution, art smuggling and industrial espionage. Sooner or later, the conflict will escalate and there will be blood. As if there weren't enough problems already with stealing blueprints from the eccentric Inventors and the increasingly violent war with the Ash and Oak Club.

Special Rules

Under Cover of Mists: There may be no more Mist Templates on the Battlefield than there are Models that can place them. When a Model places a new Mist Template, and it would exceed the maximum number of Mist Templates on the Battlefield, the Player who places the new Mist Template has to remove one of the Mist Templates. At the end of the turn Players whose models can place Mist Templates take turns to remove Mist Templates exceeding the maximum number of Mist Templates, starting with the Player who has the Initiative.

Mist Template: This Template blocks LoS through it. Models within it gain Cover [+1R]. See Mist Walker and Mistmaker.

Mistmaker: [Quick Action] Place a Mist Template in BtB with This Model.

Mist Walker: At any Moment in This Model's Movement Action, when it is completely within a Mist Template, you can place it completely in another Mist Template, then it can continue its movement. Remove the first Mist Template This Model moved from.

Concealed in the Crowd: This Model enters play with a Crowd Marker. It can only lose its Crowd Marker under one of three circumstances:

- It attacks an Enemy Model,

- It ends its Activation within 3" of an Enemy Model,

- Enemy Model ends its Activation within 3" of it.

A Model with a Crowd Marker cannot be a target of any Shooting or Melee Attack and cannot be targeted by enemy spells.

Gui Deng

HERO
Orc / 30mm

Actions	Move	Fight	Str	Guns	Reflex	Wounds
2	5	3	3	3	4	8

3

ABILITIES

Techniques of Sunnir Masters: This Model gains Protection [1] when targeted with enemy spells.

Mistmaker: [Quick Action] Place a Mist Template in BtB with This Model.

GADGETS

Lanterns of Spiritual Guidance: Whenever a Model is removed from play within 12", This Model may gain one Ability of the removed Model until end of turn.

MAGIC

Magic Ability [3]: Spiritualism

	Type	Cost	Range	S	Notes
Spirit Theft	Magic Attack	1	12"	-	*Spirit Theft*

Spirit Theft: This model gains one chosen Target Model's Ability until end of turn.

	Type	Cost	Range	S	Notes
Spirit Reflection	Magic Attack	2	12"	-	*Spirit Reflection*

Spirit Reflection: This model and one friendly Model in range and LoS gain one chosen Target Model's Ability until end of turn.

	Type	Cost	Range	S	Notes
Mind Erase	Magic Attack	1	12"	-	*Mind Erase*

Mind Erase: Target Model loses one chosen Ability until end of the Game.

"Don't think about why she's wearing that blindfold. You've heard people say that she can look into a corpse's eyes and learn how he died, haven't you? Maybe it's true... Let me just tell you what I've seen when I looked into her eyes, after losing a bet. I've seen my own death and what awaits me beyond. I'll say no more. If you're curious, you'll have to try it yourself."

The Triad thrives on mysteries, shameful secrets, and knowledge that should be left alone. Procuring information from the living is easy, but figuring out what the dead are hiding is another matter entirely. Unless, of course, one has access to the services of a talented medium. Gui Deng joined the organization as a little girl and has been helping the Triad for years by ridding spirits of their secrets. In time, she has become a confidante to lost souls from all over Lyonesse, slowly drifting away from the world of the living with each newly acquired piece of ghostly information. Today, no one knows whether Gui Deng faithfully serves the Triad, carries out her own plans, or listens to nothing but the whispers of spirits trapped in her lanterns.

TRIAD OF LOTUS DRAGON

Xen Jidao

HERO
Orc / 30mm

Actions	Move	Fight	Str	Guns	Reflex	Wounds
2	5	4	4	2	6	8

2 FUNDS

ABILITIES

Techniques of Sunnir Masters: This Model gains Protection [1] when targeted with enemy spells.

Mistmaker: [Quick Action] Place a Mist Template in BtB with This Model

GADGETS

Silk Cloth of the Dragon Order: +1R (inculded in the profile).

MAGIC

Magic Ability [4]: Spiritualism

	Type	Cost	Range	Notes
Mistification	Buff [1]	0	6"	*Mistwalk*

Mistwalk: Target Model gains Mistwalker until the end of this turn.

	Type	Cost	Range	Notes
Mind Control	Attack	1	18"	*Mind Control*

Mind Control: Target enemy Henchman makes one Action as if it was a friendly Model immediately after This Model's Activation.

	Type	Cost	Range	S	Notes
Ki Strike	Projectile	1	12"	6	*Topple*

Topple: Model hit is Toppled.

"You ask if we have the right to treat Liao Nesse as our playground? We come from the Dragon Empire – the center of the world, culture of which lasts ceaselessly for five thousand years. Now look at those long nosed barbarians and their confused young queen. Turning this city into our colony is not our right. It is our duty. Observe."

"Listen to your opponent's breath. When he attacks – evade, and when he stumbles under his own weight – strike."

Xen Jidao treats Lyonesse like a mahjong board. He is as old as the mountains, as sly as a fox and as patient as a turtle. He leads the Triad of Lotus Dragon with imperturbable calm, knowing that hundreds of generations of orkish sages stand behind his every decision. He disdains western technology, ignores all aspects of modernity, and ventures outside of Pothill's Shang-Town only in a tightly curtained litter. Only one thing remains a secret: why did Xen Jidao leave the Dragon Empire he loves so much?

TRIAD OF LOTUS DRAGON

	Mr. Cheng	Actions	Move	Fight	Str	Guns	Reflex	Wounds
	HERO Orc / 30mm	2	5	2	3	2	4	10

ABILITIES

Acidic Fumes: Models passing through or starting their Activations in Mist Templates within 12" of Mr Cheng suffer the Effect of an Acid Template. Models cannot Mistwalk through these Templates.

Acid Template: Effect: This Model suffers 2 Acid Damage. If it has any Armor (but not Acid Resistance) it is reduced by 2 until end of turn.

Dark Energy: When Mr. Cheng has 14 or more W, he gains +2 to F, S and R. When he has 21+ W, he gains +5 to F, S and R instead.

Power of Blood: At the beginning of This Model's Activation, you may have This Model lose 2 Wounds to gain 1 Magic Ability. This Model may have no more than 5 Magic Ability.

GADGETS

Ring of Ichiko: Confers Magic Ability [2]: Ritualism

Jade Amulet: This Model cannot be the target of spells.

MAGIC

	Type	Cost	Range	S	Notes
Leech Soul	Projectile	1	12"	5	*Leech Soul*

Leech Soul: This Model gains Wounds equal to Wounds lost by the Target Model. This model may have more Wounds than it started with.

	Type	Cost	Range	Notes
Bloodboil	Attack/Buff [1]	0	6"	*Bloodboil*

Bloodboil: Target Model loses 2 W but gains +2S and +2F until end of turn.

"Look at this city. A huge pile of dung, on which people keep jumping at each others throats. Whoever brings the others down and climbs through their corpses towards fame and fortune gets to live. It is a place more sinister than the steamy jungles of Sunnir. More treacherous than the muddy depths of Dragon River. More deadly than the shark-riddled canals of Zhonglung. Only one devoid of scruples will get to survive here. I love Lyonesse. That old fool Jidao fails to realize the gravity of the situation."

"The Fog in Lyonesse really is a gate to another world, but only a madman would dare to cross its threshold. To follow the paths though the Fog is to enter the territory of the Fae and the Lyonesse ghosts, and we are not yet ready for this encounter. Understand that I'm not poisoning the Fog with black lotus magic to punish you. I'm doing it for your own good. When the wounds heal, you will surely understand."

Although born in the Old Country, Mr Cheng spent his childhood and youth in the Bridgebank slums. He dresses in a western fashion and understands the needs of the Lyonesse poor like no one else. His network manages illegal lotus dens, houses of ill repute disguised as massage parlors and antique shops serving as fronts for moneylenders and fences. No one is in any doubt that the position of Lotus Dragon has been considerably strengthened since Mr Cheng joined the ranks of the triad. Also, no one is in any doubt that Mr Cheng is loyal to only one person. Mr Cheng.

Wandering Actor

HERO
Orc / 30mm

Actions	Move	Fight	Str	Guns	Reflex	Wounds
2	5	2	3	2	4	8

5 FUNDS

ABILITIES

Techniques of Sunnir Masters: This Model gains Protection [1] when targeted with enemy spells.

Concealed in the Crowd: This Model enters play with a Crowd Marker. It can only lose its Crowd Marker under one of three circumstances:

• It attacks an Enemy Model,

• It ends its Activation within 3" of an Enemy Model,

• Enemy Model ends its Activation within 3" of it.

A Model with a Crowd Marker cannot be a target of any Shooting or Melee Attack and cannot be targeted by enemy spells.

All Suits: Wandering Actor can use cards in any suit while making a Heroic Move or Heroic Recovery. This Model may not discard cards to boost Activating Objectives.

True Identity: At the beginning of a game turn, if you have any dead Hero Models, you can make This Model reveal his true identity. Discard a card of the suit of the dead Hero you want This Model to change into, then remove This Model from the battlefield and replace it with the dead Hero Model. The replacing Hero Model is treated as a new Model that just entered play.

"The first mask signifies a young man, the second – a bearded man, third – a mighty warrior, fourth – a scholarly beardless warrior. You must learn to distinguish between them at first glance. Your life may depend on it. "

"A traditional Shangese proverb says: one who focuses on masks forgets that a face hides behind them."

The traditional Shangese opera from Zhonglung is an art with a centuries-old tradition – subtle, sophisticated and completely incomprehensible to an average citizen of Lyonesse. Only in the Shangese district do the actors enjoy their deserved popularity and fame. They can also be encountered outside of Pothill, although most passers-by treat them like common street musicians, or simply ignore. This often turns out to be a serious mistake.

TRIAD OF LOTUS DRAGON

Phoenix	Actions	Move	Fight	Str	Guns	Reflex	Wounds
HERO Orc / 30mm	2	5	6	7	3	4	9

1

ABILITIES

Techniques of Sunnir Masters: This Model gains Protection [1] when targeted with enemy spells.

GADGETS

Fire Sabre: Melee Weapon, +3S (included in profile), Armor Piercing [1].

Firecracker: Ranged Weapon.

	S	0-12"	Notes
Firecracker	4	0	Fire, *Instant*

Instant: You may use this ability at the end of every Action, even if This Model had made another Action or is in BtB with an enemy Model.

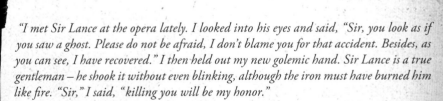

"I met Sir Lance at the opera lately. I looked into his eyes and said, "Sir, you look as if you saw a ghost. Please do not be afraid, I don't blame you for that accident. Besides, as you can see, I have recovered." I then held out my new golemic hand. Sir Lance is a true gentleman – he shook it without even blinking, although the iron must have burned him like fire. "Sir," I said, "killing you will be my honor."

"The Empress has sent me to observe the people of the West, learn their customs and to bring that knowledge back to the Forbidden City. I shall fulfill this mission and more – I will bring the secrets of their technology inside my body. It is rightly said that a phoenix is the Empress' favorite bird."

Phoenix was born in the forges of Blackstone when the dwarven technomancers brought his soul back to a body animated with golemic implants. In the previous life he was an informal ambassador of the Empress. The less subtle would simply call him a spy. Whatever his duties, they led to a duel with Lord Oakroot. A duel, which ended with an unfortunate accident involving a steamroller, and in effect led to Phoenix's rebirth. Though iron discipline and toilsome training, Phoenix regained the full use of his limbs, and goes back into action stronger than ever before.

Ata Kijao	Actions	Move	Fight	Str	Guns	Reflex	Wounds
HERO Orc / 30mm	2	5	3	3	5	5	6

n/a FUNDS

ABILITIES

Techniques of Sunnir Masters: This Model gains Protection [1] when targeted with enemy spells.

Mistress of Concealment: This Model doubles the advantages of Cover it is in. For example, if it is in Cover [1] it counts as being in Cover [2].

Retreat to Shadows: If This Model kills an enemy Model in its Action, at the end of this Action it can be placed anywhere on the battlefield completely within a Mist Template.

Mistmaker: [Quick Action] Place a Mist Template in BtB with This Model.

GADGETS

Shuriken: Ranged Weapon.

	S	8"	Notes
Shuriken	3	0	Quick, Fastshot[2], Gruesome Damage

TRIAD OF LOTUS DRAGON

"Don't laugh, Bob, I'm telling you – the triads have demons in their service. Black Pete suckered them out of their lotus, and he croaked a week later. They found him in his room. Something gutted him like a fish, and all the locks were shut. From the inside! His neighbors saw smoke coming from under the door and called the guards. Was it not for that clogged up stove, he'd be lying there to this day and not a soul would notice. Demons, I tell you. Shangese demons."

"(Silence. Sound of a drawn sword. Sound of a falling body. Silence.)"

Ata Kijao is a living legend. Few know of her existence, and not many of them dare to speak of it. Allegedly, she trained at a monastery hidden among the glaciers in the Telogans. It is said that she is the Empress' thirteenth granddaughter, that she casts no shadow and steps so lightly, that even smoke and fog carry her. It is known that she is as quick as a thought, fights like a demon and no one alive has ever heard her voice.

Triad of Lotus Dragon
HENCHMAN

Shadow	Actions	Move	Fight	Str	Guns	Reflex	Wounds
HENCHMAN Orc / 30mm	2	5	3	3	3	4	8

COST 2

ABILITIES

Concealment Art Adept: When in Cover [1], This Model is treated as in Cover [2].

GADGETS

Repeater Crossbow: Ranged Weapon.

	S	0-12”	12-24”	24-36”	Notes
Repeater Crossbow	4	+1	0	-2	**Armor Piercing [3]**

"A good warrior knows how to exploit the strength of his opponent. Look at that repeater crossbow. We shall turn their own technology against them."

Fanatic triad warriors, skilled in traditional martial arts and armed with modern pneumatic repeater crossbows. Fast like the wind, quiet as shadows. Xen Jidao and Mr Cheng both consider forming the shade squads to be their personal success.

Fisherman	Actions	Move	Fight	Str	Guns	Reflex	Wounds
HENCHMAN Orc / 30mm	2	5	3	4	3	4	8

COST 1

ABILITIES

Concealed in the Crowd: This Model enters play with a Crowd Marker. It can only lose its Crowd Marker under one of three circumstances:

- It attacks an Enemy Model,

- It ends its Activation within 3" of an Enemy Model,

- Enemy Model ends its Activation within 3" of it.

A Model with a Crowd Marker cannot be a target of any Shooting or Melee Attack and cannot be targeted by enemy spells.

GADGETS

Fishing Net: Ranged Weapon.

	S	2"	Notes
Fishing Net	0	0	*Quick, Topple*

Fishing net doesn't deal any damage. Instead, the Model hit is *Toppled*.

"You know, Bob, you can laugh at the orks fishing in the Tether, with their straw little boats and bamboo fishing rods. Let me tell you, though – last month, when a young leviathan lost its way and swam up the river to the docks near Pothill, they killed and stripped it to bare bones in just a couple of hours. On these straw little boats of theirs."

Nobody pays any attention to the old fishermen sitting around by the waterfront, or to the salesmen of oysters, eels and fried lobster. They are, after all, just fishermen. If people knew how huge the fish swimming in the old country's Dragon River are, and how strong the Shangese nets are, they would be more respectful towards the orkish fishermen. Usually they have to learn respect the harder way.

TRIAD OF LOTUS DRAGON

Trader	Actions	Move	Fight	Str	Guns	Reflex	Wounds
HENCHMAN Orc / 30mm	2	5	3	3	3	4	8

Cost 1

ABILITIES

Concealed in the Crowd: This Model enters play with a Crowd Marker. It can only lose its Crowd Marker under one of three circumstances:

• It attacks an Enemy Model,

• It ends its Activation within 3" of an Enemy Model,

• Enemy Model ends its Activation within 3" of it.

A Model with a Crowd Marker cannot be a target of any Shooting or Melee Attack and cannot be targeted by enemy spells.

Mistmaker: [Quick Action] Place a Mist Template in BtB with This Model

"Hey lady! Want some fried rice? Maybe won-ton soup? No? How about fireworks?"

The peddling traders are a regular part of the street panorama in the Shangese district. They sell everything to everyone, all day and night. They are everywhere and there are thousands of them. Any of them could be a triad spy, a disguised messenger, a fence, or a partisan sent on an important mission. It is good to remember that during the next visit to Pothill.

PHOENIX

MR CHENG

WANDERING ACTOR

SHADOW

ORC TRADERS

ATA KIJAO

XEN JIDAO

ORC FISHERMAN

UBUME BOREI AND WARASHI

Character Creation Rules

These rules are intended to allow you to create and develop your own characters for Wolsung Skirmish game. You can either play the game with the named characters we present you in the Clubs section, just your own custom-created characters, or a mix of both. It is however recommended that you use the same number of named and custom characters as your Opponent(s).

How to create your own Hero?

First, choose a club you want to play with. Check the races available for the club, then choose one of them for your Hero. Some races may have special rules or limitations in certain clubs. When you have chosen a race for your Hero, check his Basic Profile (see opposite).

This is a starting profile for every Human Hero. See the golden coin with a number? These are the Funds for your Hero – they stand for his overall wealth, fame or connections. These are the points with which he pays for his gadgets, henchmen and skills. Every Hero also has a Racial Ability, which is common to almost every Hero of this race. All right, don't let your Hero run around naked! He will need some magical gadgets and Heroic abilities to make fame in Lyonesse.

Every Hero must have exactly one profession chosen from the four available for each club (see pages 101-105). The profession defines the card suit the Model has. You may have more than one Hero with the same profession in your club. The gadgets and abilities are organised into Racial and Club pools.

• The Racial pool is available for every Hero of their race, no matter what Club he's in.

• The Club pool is available for every Hero in the Club, no matter his race, but are not available to a member of any other Club (unless noted otherwise).

Gadgets are further divided into types: Armor, Trinket, Ranged Weapon, Melee Weapon. If no type is given, the gadget is not considered to be of any specific type and can be mixed freely with other gadgets.

When choosing Gadgets for your Heroes you must obey all the following rules:

• Each Gadget (either Racial or Club) can only be chosen once in a Club, unless it is 'common'.

• You may have more than one of the same 'common' gadget in a club, but not on a single character.

• When two Heroes have the same 'common' gadget, they may never share other 'common' gadget.

• One Hero may never have more than one Gadget of certain type, for example Armor or Ranged Weapon.

All right, now let's see this on an example:

"I am fielding an Ash and Oak Club and I've chosen Human for the race of my Hero. I have the basic 6 Funds, with which I buy a profession for two Funds and a gadget for 3 Funds. I'll leave the remaining 1 point of Funds and add it to the clubs Funds Pool."

The Heroes you create form the unchanging core of your club's list. They may gain funds, abilities and gadgets, but the only way to remove a Hero from a list is to cross him off and replace with a newly created one. The funds pool may be used to recruit Henchmen and buy new gadgets and abilities for your Heroes. Once a gadget is bought it cannot be removed or sold back. Henchmen can be fired giving full refund between games and you may recruit fresh Henchmen freely before each game, with only two constraints:

• You may never field more Henchmen than twice the number of Heroes you field.

• The funds pool cannot be lower than 0.

Fantasy races and nationalities

All the countries in Vanadia are multiracial and concepts like „the Elven language" do not exist. Fellow countrymen of different races who live in the same area and speak the same language share a much stronger bond than members of the same race who belong to two quarreling nations and cannot communicate without an interpreter.

Human

Hero / 30mm

Actions	Move	Fight	Str	Guns	Reflex	Wounds
2	5	3	3	3	3	9

6 FUNDS

RACIAL ABILITY

Beginner's Luck: Once per game This Model may Re-roll all the dice it rolled in a single Test.

GADGETS

Hidden Umbrella Blade: [1], common. +1F

Brass knuckles: [1], common. +1S

Fitzgerald's Hunting Monocle: [1], common. +1G

Doc Anna's Pain Relief: [1], common. +3W

Uncle Hoggart's Pigeon Gun: [1], common. Ranged Weapon.

Name	S	0-8"	8-16"	16-24"	Notes
Uncle Hoggart's Pigeon Gun	4	+1	-1	-2	Quick

Buzzardo's Hunting Rifle: [2], Ranged Weapon.

Name	S	0-12"	12-24"	24-36"	Notes
Buzzardo's Hunting Rifle	8	0	-1	-2	Move Penalty [1], Armor Piercing [3]

Humans are a very diverse race. Depending on the place of origin, their skin color may vary from white to dark brown. They usually have green, celadon, or dark blue eyes, but not always. Even eyes of a dark brown color tend to have a hint of green – much like water in a muddy river.

Humans are indeed like water in a way, finding its way into every crevice and collecting all the scummy dirt in the process. Because of their diverse nature, they do not fit any stereotype. To look at it from a different angle, one could say that there is at least one human to be found for every stereotype.

In Vanadia, humans are the driving force behind the middle class: members of liberal professions, followers of new trends, and travelers who bring exotic souvenirs from faraway lands. Many of them are sailors, travelers, and explorers. Human tribes can also be found in the deserts of Lemuria and Sunnir, in the Atlantean jungles, and the prairies of Vinland. They never constitute a majority on any of the continents.

Humans are restless. Ever curious of what lies beyond the horizon and where each path leads, always being tempted by the call of the unknown. That is why they can be easily persuaded to partake in any sort of mad endeavor if one takes advantage of their intrinsic curiosity.

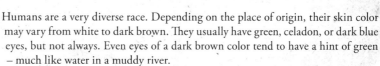

CHARACTER CREATION RULES

Elf

Hero / 30mm

Actions	Move	Fight	Str	Guns	Reflex	Wounds
2	6	4	2	3	4	9

Wolson 5 Funds

Racial Ability

Hypnotic Aura: Models may not Fence when being attacked in Melee by an Elf.

Gadgets

Silk Duelling Gloves: [1], common. +1F

Fitzgerald's Hunting Monocle: [1], common. +1G

Super Comfort Suit by Marco&Girardo: [1], +1R

Harper's Crafted Dueling Sword: [3], Melee Weapon. +3F

Tall and slender, the elves have slightly pointed ears, huge, expressive almond-shaped eyes, thin noses, and tiny white teeth. Elven women usually have slight builds, as ampler shapes are considered plebeian. This makes men and women relatively similar in terms of appearance. Elves have mostly fair hair: from white, through pale blue and gold, to light brown and green. They usually have no facial hair. Ginger or black hair or beards are an oddity and a strong sign of having humans or trolls for ancestors.

With age, elves get more and more detached from the physical world and drift into their memories and intricate daydreaming. Eventually, aging elves lose their way back, their minds floating away to the land of dreams, their bodies falling into a deep sleep from which they usually never wake up. It is said that some elves pass through to the other side, fully disappearing from the physical world. The oldest families in Alfheim have crypts that house their dreaming ancestors, who supposedly date back to the times of caesars.

It is worth noting that elves have blue blood. Literally.

For centuries, almost every Vanadian aristocrat was an elf. These proportions have shifted somewhat nowadays, but it is still uncommon to meet an elf who does not come from some wealthy, respectable family with deep roots and traditions dating back to the ancient past.

Vanadia is the cradle of the elvenkind. In the colonial era, however, they began to settle all over the world, taking their customs and lifestyle with them to overseas lands. The only elven tribe residing outside of Vanadia – the olive-skinned, dark-haired Yakshas – lives in Dekan.

There is a dark side to the staunch conservatism of the elven families – in the rapidly changing social structure, the race is growing increasingly irrelevant. The period of ceaseless domination seems to be ending for this race, and it appears there is nothing that could change that.

The elves' great weakness is their extraordinary vulnerability to iron. Rashes and other allergic reactions caused by handling iron tools or traveling by an old train can make life difficult. The real threat, however, are wounds inflicted with iron weapons.

Orc

Hero / 30mm

Actions	Move	Fight	Str	Guns	Reflex	Wounds
2	5	4	3	3	4	8

5 Funds

RACIAL ABILITY

Techniques of Sunnir Masters: This Model gains Protection [+1R] when targeted with enemy spells.

GADGETS

Shanginian Fighting Bands: [1], common. +1F

Twinkle's Elixir of Strength: [1], common. +1S

Kiochi's Silk kimono: [1], +1R

Boots of Swift Movement: [1], +1M

Repeater Crossbow: [3], Ranged Weapon.

Name	S	0-12"	12-24"	24-36"	Notes
Repeater Crossbow	3	+1	0	-2	Armor Piercing [2], Fastshot [2]

Depending on their place of birth, orcs significantly differ in terms of appearance. They are usually taller than humans, although exceptions to that rule do apply. Their distinctive features are protruding cheekbones, almond-shaped, piercing eyes, slightly tipped ears, flat noses, and strong jaws with slightly pronounced fangs. The skin color varies between Sunnirian yellow, Atteman olive, Vindian red, and the ebony of the Lemurian warriors. Most orcs have raven-black hair – curly in Lemuria and Atteman, and straight in Sunnir.

Due to the still dominant standard of Vanadian beauty set by elves, orcish men are not considered very handsome. Women, on the other hand, are known for their fiery temperament and can easily make many any gentleman's heart race.

It is hard to summarize a race that spawned both the Lemurian cannibal tribes and the sophisticated ancient civilization of Shang-In. All orcs have a deep connection with the spirit world, and the ability to see the past by gazing into the eyes of the dead. They remain in touch with their ancestral spirits.

Most orcs live outside of Vanadia – in Sunnir, Vinland, and Lemuria, where their societies are governed by their own laws. In Sunnir, orcs mostly play the part of the aristocracy, similarly to the Vanadian elves. Their situation has started to change with the dawn of the colonial era: Vanadian citizens have started exploring cultures previously alien to them, and more and more young orcs have started to attend Vanadian universities, having permanently moved to the Old Continent.

Despite this, the orcs in Vanadia remain strangers. Even if they are born there, some nuances of Vanadian culture still remain a mystery to them.

Troll

Hero / 30mm

Actions	Move	Fight	Str	Guns	Reflex	Wounds
2	5	3	5	3	3	10

5 FUNDS

RACIAL ABILITY

Fiery Passion: This Model has Resistance to Fire [3].

GADGETS

Magical Warpaint: [1], common. +1F

Mechanic Biceps: [1], common. +1S

Margini's Potion of Swiftness: [1], +1R

Olglaf's Arcane Two-Handed Mace: [2], Melee Weapon. +1F +1S

Steam Powered Limb Replacement: [1], common. +3W

Bulletproof Suit: [2], common. Armor [3]

Young trolls look a bit like wild animal cubs, with their distinctive large eyes, pointed ears and sharp teeth. They behave like them, too. Adult trolls are tall and powerfully built. Despite their sharp facial features and a fiery look, they are considered ugly. Wild, red hair is very common. Old trolls eventually become monsters with muscles as strong as steel, thick, growth-ridden skin, sharp claws, and drooling fangs. As they get older, they grow progressively bigger, reaching a size far beyond the capabilities of other races.

The changes that occur in the bodies and minds of trolls with age are colossal. Young, adult, and old trolls are basically three separate species. Self-reliant since early childhood, young trolls begin to grow rapidly upon reaching puberty, only to fall victim to irreversible degeneration as years go by. In their seventies, they are no more than bloodthirsty beasts. Nobody knows the lifespan of a troll, since most of them commit suicide before utterly losing control over their actions. Those that do not, end up killed by their kin, or the authorities.

Trolls have forged a unique mentality and code of conduct. Their main goal in life is to leave a mark on the world – to earn immortality though outstanding achievements. Recklessly brave and ruthlessly ambitious, their careers are bright and brief, like a sudden flame. That is not just an empty metaphor, as some trolls possess the ability to reach into their internal flames in order to protect themselves from actual fire and heat, or to provoke others into a sudden, uncontrolled outburst of emotion.

Trolls are aware that they have little time to leave their mark on the world, which is why many of them perform their tasks with obsessive dedication. The word of such trolls is sacred. Once they undertake something, they will not rest until they fulfill their obligation.

Vanadian trolls come from Hrimthorst. Wild troll tribes can be found in the jungles of Lemuria, plateaus of Atlantis, and plains of Sunnir.

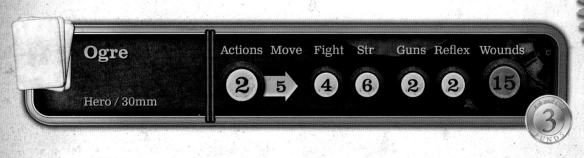

Ogre

Hero / 30mm

Actions	Move	Fight	Str	Guns	Reflex	Wounds
2	5	4	6	2	2	15

3

RACIAL ABILITY

Hard to Kill: If This Model's Wounds are reduced to 0 and it had more than 1 Wound at the moment it suffered damage, it is reduced to 1 Wound instead.

GADGETS

Rokgor's Boxing Gloves: [1], +1F, +1S

Steam Powered Limb Replacement: [1], common. +3W

Bowler Hat of Protection: [2], common. Armor [3]

Ogres are huge. They are taller and have a more powerful build than adult trolls. It is said that they are animals almost as much as people. Hairy, with disproportionately long arms, pronounced fangs, and heavily protruding brow ridges, they resemble giant apes more than sentient beings.

Be it due to some kind of divine curse or nature's whim, there are no ogre females – every member of this race is male. Luckily for them, they have that certain spark that makes them fascinating and irresistible to women of other races. If a boy is born out of such a relationship, he will always be an ogre, whilst the few baby girls will be the same race as the mother.

In this era of hypocrisy, buttoned-up collars, and long dresses, the exuberant, spontaneous and impressively strong ogres possess a certain „something." Many highborn ladies take a long look at them and begin to wonder how exactly a pale, delicate elf or a cold fish of a dwarf is somehow more appealing.

Due to social pressure, baby ogres are usually rejected by their mothers and end up in orphanages, growing up to be laborers, servants, or petty criminals. The only race that does not see a problem with ogres are halflings – ogre children are treated like any other and are raised to be respectable members of the family.

The stereotype of an ogre servant is deeply ingrained in society. Times are changing, however, and the status of ogres is changing along with them.

More and more members of this race have lately actively begun to fight for a better place in society. One just has to go through the morning papers to see how many film stars, sportsmen, and police officers are ogres. The gossip section is also quite enlightening. Unusual marriages, surprising rulings on inheritance cases, or heirs to great fortunes being found in ogrish orphanages – these are all increasingly common occurrences.

There are tribes living in the northern plains, whose men are mostly ogres.

CHARACTER CREATION RULES

Gnome	Actions	Move	Fight	Str	Guns	Reflex	Wounds
Hero / 30mm	2	5	3	3	3	3	9

Wolsung 5 FUNDS

RACIAL ABILITY

Natural Engineer: Action, Once per game: Place a Golem Servant model in BtB with This Model.

Scientist: This Model provides a Control Range for Golems.

GADGETS

Issue of "Ritualism Weekly": [1], common. Add +1 to Magic Ability.

Margini's Potion of Swiftness: [1], +1R

Technomage Apparel: [2], Gains MA [4]: Technomagic and spell Lightning.

	Type	Cost	Range	S	Notes
Lightning	Projectile	0	12"	3	

Gnomes are small and spry. They are about as tall as halflings, though much leaner in comparison. They most resemble dwarves with a slimmer build. Gnomes are traditionally pictured as little people with long beards wearing distinctive black and red clothes. Nowadays, more and more gnomes tend to dress in accordance with popular fashion, although very few choose to shave off their mustaches.

Gnomes are a mysterious and secretive race. They have been living outside the rest of society for centuries, isolated in their world of obscure customs and traditions. They stick together more than the other races, often constituting a separate nation within a nation. Gnomish politicians or generals are rather unheard of, but every educated individual is able to name at least a few of their mages, scientists, and inventors. Despite staying on the sidelines – or perhaps because of it – gnomes often evoke resentment or even outright hostility. And nobody is really sure how much truth there is to the rumors of their dark rituals.

Most gnomes belong to the middle or lower class, but each of them received a thorough basic education back at home. According to their beliefs, it was gnomes who invented writing. The most honored members of their walled-in community are wise men called godi, who study the old legends and are appointed keepers of the race's entire history. Most of them are skilled at writing runes and building technomagical golems.

Gnomes come from Thule, an island on the Sea of Ice. Their turbulent past has scattered them all over Vanadia – from the icy Hrimthorst, through sunny Coriole and the misty isles of the United Kingdom, to the frozen tundras of Morgovia. Clusters of gnomes can also be found in every major colony, from Vinland to the islands of Shang-Dekan.

Despite living in Vanadia for centuries, gnomes remain alien and foreign. They stand out with their customs, religion, knowledge and magic that is inaccessible to other races. They are secretive and keep to themselves. It is hardly surprising that gnomes are often met with barely concealed distrust, and every tense social situation turns into quite an ordeal for them.

Halfling

Hero / 30mm

Actions	Move	Fight	Str	Guns	Reflex	Wounds
2	6	2	1	3	5	7

RACIAL ABILITY

Swift: This Model may always use their Reflex instead of Fight when Parrying in Melee. It also automatically passes the test to Leave Melee.

GADGETS

Margini's Potion of Swiftness: [1], +1R

Blackmarket map of Lyonesse's Tunnels: [2], This Model gains Infiltration.

Peruzzi's Pocket Crossbow: [1], common. Ranged Weapon.

Name	S	0-6"	6-12"	Notes
Peruzzi's Pocket Crossbow	2	+2	+1	Quick, Fastshot [2]

Halflings are usually just over three feet tall, with human body proportions and thick curly hair. Men tend to sport impressive sideburns, which is an element of fashion virtually independent of their country of origin. The color of their eyes and hair varies: it is equally as easy to spot a swarthy, dark-haired halfling as one that is a pale, freckled ginger.

Halflings have always been associated with farming, big families, and idyllic country life. With the dawn of the Magical-Industrial Revolution, however, this image started to fade, being replaced with a new stereotype: a lower-class street-smart con man with sticky fingers.

While halflings are biologically capable of living longer than humans, the environment plays a huge part in their lifespan. Factory workers toiling 14 hours a day can expect to live no longer than the human average of 30 years.

There have been many changes to the countryside after the War. Small farms have ceased to be profitable and entire multigenerational halfling families had to move to the cities in order to make a living. Wrenched away from their native environment and devoid of their relatives' support, they quickly blended in the anonymous crowd of workers, craftsmen, and petty criminals. The traditional system of values based on multigenerational families simply could not have survived in the big cities, in the cramped confines of tenement houses. Deprived of their tradition, halflings are either slowly pushed to the margins of society, or seek shelter in organized crime.

Apart from Vanadia, halfling communities can be encountered in the fertile valleys and large river deltas of Lemuria and Atlantis.

Halflings are famous for their great spirit residing in admittedly small bodies. This may prove to be an issue when faced against brute force – courage, cunning and good reflexes help to put up a fight and avoid blows, but are not of much use when the opponent's hit actually connects.

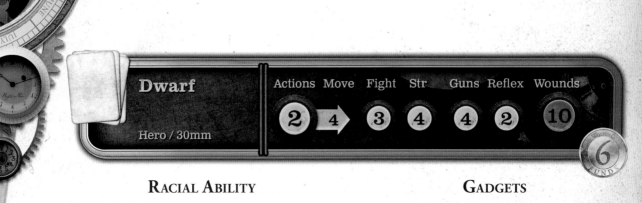

Dwarf		Actions	Move	Fight	Str	Guns	Reflex	Wounds	
Hero / 30mm		2	4	3	4	4	2	10	6

RACIAL ABILITY

Night Vision: This Model may trace LoS through Smoke Templates and ignores Low Visibility.

GADGETS

Hidden Umbrella Blade: [1], common. +1F

Mechanic Biceps: [1], common. +1S

Gwiddle's Prototype Optic Sight: [1], common. +1G

Super Comfort Suit by Marco&Girardo: [1], +1R

Steam Powered Limb Replacement: [1], common. +3W

Finger Pistol: [1], common. Ranged Weapon.

Name	S	0-8"	8-16"	16-24"	Notes
Finger Pistol	4	+1	-1	-2	Quick

Although dwarves are rarely taller than a meter and a half, they tend to be much stronger and tougher than the average human. They usually have dark to black hair and sport bushy beards, which strongly contrasts with their distinctive fair complexion. Members of this race are accustomed to the underground darkness and prefer to avoid the sun, to which their skin is extremely sensitive.

Dwarves are famous for their self-control and sincerity. They see the world as a complicated, quantifiable mechanism that can be taken apart and analyzed in a logical fashion. The earthen folk trust cold reason, not fleeting emotions.

Dwarves have an inborn knack for working with machines, and display unusual tolerance for golemic and mechanical implants.

Dwarves have always been associated with mining, metallurgy, and commerce. They usually work as mechanics, miners, engineers, or laborers. There are also many famous dwarven inventors, investors, factory owners, and bankers. In some countries, dwarven clans constitute the core of the aristocracy. Those who have chosen a military career serve in heavy infantry, armored divisions, or sapper squads, many also holding high positions as officers.

It is unknown whether the mountains of Vanadia or the mighty peaks of central Sunnir are the cradle of this race. What is certain is that they can be encountered basically everywhere, apart from Lemuria and Atlantis.

Dwarves have been living underground and leading a mostly nocturnal lifestyle since time immemorial. Their eyes have huge pupils and lack irises. In conjunction with their marble-white complexion makes functioning in daylight difficult for them.

CHARACTER CREATION RULES

Ash and Oak Club

Every Hero Model in the Ash and Oak Club gains a passive ability "Noble":

Noble: This is a keyword used to make other rules work with it. If a model has a Noble rule it is considered a Noble model and rules that require a Noble Model as a subject work with it.

Allergy to iron: Elves cannot choose any Armor.

Alfish: Elves pay [1] for their profession rather than [2].

Races Available:

Human, Elf, Orc, Troll, Ogre, Gnome, Dwarf and Halfling.

Club Gadgets and professions

Professions:

Man About Town: Cost [2] Common. Hearts. +1R, may draw 2 cards and discard one each time it's Activated.

Duellist Extraordinaire: Cost [2] Common. Spades. +1F, may re-roll one F die each Action.

War Hero: Cost [2] Common. Diamonds. May add cards in any colour for Heroic Action, and may add cards even after passing. Heroic Recovery without discarding a card.

Famous Explorer: Cost [2] Common. Clubs. +3W, Armor [1], Heroic Move without discarding a card.

Gadgets:

Ranged Weapons:

Windbüchse Cost [2], Ranged Weapon

Name	S	0-12"	12-24"	24-36"	Notes
Windbüchse	3	'+1	0	-1	Small Calibre

Galvanic Rifle Cost [2], Ranged Weapon

Name	S	0-12"	12-24"	24-48"	Notes
Galvanic Rifle	4	0	-1	-2	Move, Penalty [1], **Armor** Piercing [4]

Harquebus Cost [2], Ranged Weapon

Name	S	0-6"	6-12"	12-18"	Notes
Harquebus	8	'+1	-2	-3	Move Penalty [1], Fire

Colt Navy: Cost [2], Ranged Weapon

Name	S	0-8"	8-16"	16-24"	Notes
Colt Navy	4	„+"1	-1	-2	Quick, Fast Shot [2]

Melee Weapons:

Golf bag: Cost [2], Melee Weapon

- Lob: Ranged Attack, 12" R, does not require LoS, instead of suffering damage the Target Model is toppled.

A Model needs to be in contact with terrain to claim cover against this shot

May also choose to use one bat in melee per Activation:

- Driver: instead of suffering damage the Target Model is toppled

- 3 wood: +2S

- Putter: +2F

[1] cost gadgets:

Dog Whistle: Cost [1], Once per game. Action. Place 2 Hounds in BtB with This Model. Activate the Hounds immediately after This Model ends it's Activation. In further turns Activate the Hounds normally. Hunting Pack: Both of This Model's Hounds must remain within 6" of one another, and are Activated at the same time. For the purposes of multiple combat, move all the hounds first, then split the combat, then fight in melee.

Balloon: Cost [1], *Arriving somewhat late, but in extraordinary style, the character swoops from the skies in a graceful balloon!* This Model gains the Infiltrator special rule.

Formal attire : Cost [1], With his (or her) nose in the air, the character keeps on with his business, ignoring plebeian plaints. Once per game: You may Steal the First Player's Initiative or make an Additional Activation choosing a card after all other Players revealed theirs. If you do so, This Model has to be chosen to Activate.

Nose like no other: Cost [1], *With his (or her) widely branched genealogical tree, being kindred to most of the noble families, the character is almost guaranteed to meet a collateral relative in even the weirdest places.* At the beginning of the game choose one enemy Model. This Model and the chosen Model cannot attack each other in any way.

Carefree bigwig: Cost [1], *Disregarding boring tactical approach, the character acts when he (or she) sees fit. No one can argue though, as whenever he acts, he surpasses everybody!* This gadget can be used once per game, at the beginning of a turn. This Model then gains +1A but is also Mindless until end of this turn.

Umbrella: Cost [1], This Model gains +1F and +1R if targeted by a living Model from 12" or less.

Military Experience: Cost [1], Friendly Noble Models benefit from +1G while within 6" and Line of Sight of This Model.

Dearest Employer: Cost [1], Friendly Henchmen have +1F and +1G if they are within 6" and Line of Sight of This Model.

The Most Noble Order of the Garter: Cost [1], The character is the toughest, hardiest explorer of jungles, deserts and ballrooms alike. The Model is Hard To Kill.

Armor:

Hidden Armor: Cost [1], *Safety first.* The Model has Armor [2]

[2] Cost gadgets

Subscription of "Gentleman's Guide to Technology": Cost [2], The character gets new gadgets regularly as a part of the subscription. At the start of the first game turn, discard a card to choose a gadget from the following list:

Court card of spades: Stasis Bubble

Court card of hearts: Time Warp Generator

Court card of diamonds: Personal Phaser

Court card of clubs: Compact Matter Shifter

Stasis Bubble [Gadget - subscribers only]: One use only. Action. Place 3" Stasis Template centered over the Model Activating this Gadget. Until the end of turn no Model may move into the Template and the Model Activating the Gadget is no longer considered as participating in Melee. Models that start their Activation within the Stasis Template must declare a Move Action as their first Action and cannot end their Action inside the area of the Template. Stasis Template does not block LoS or provide cover however any magical or non-magical ranged attack tracing LoS through the marker has its S reduced by 4 to a minimum of 1. If a toppled Model starts its Activation inside the Template it must stand up first and then has to use a Move to leave the Template if it has any Actions left.

Time Warp Generator [Gadget - subscribers only]: One use only. The Gadget may be used at the beginning of equipped Model's Activation. Until end of turn the Model may perform only Move Actions but doubles its basic M and R.

Personal Phaser [Gadget - subscribers only]: The Model may use this device during his Activation declaring a special Move Action. Mark 3 points anywhere on the table and at least 6" from each other and make a Reflex test. For each success rolled your Opponent nominates a marker that the Model may be placed on. If no marker is left - your Opponent chooses the direction and the Model using the device is moved up to his normal Move in the direction chosen. If he contacts any other Model, terrain or the table edge he stops immediately.

Compact Matter Shifter [Gadget - subscribers only]: Ranged Weapon. If you hit the target, instead of causing damage roll a D6 and move Target Model up to the distance rolled in the direction chosen ignoring any terrain. The Model may end this Move in BtB with enemy Model. There must be a place for the Model's base at the end of this move. You may target your own Model with this weapon. In that case target's R is reduced to 0 until end of this Action.

Spells:

A purse of gold: Cost [1], Magic Ability [4]

	Type	Cost	Range	S	Notes
A purse of gold	Magic Attack	0	18"	-	Mind Control

Mind Control: The target of this spell can be any opposing living Henchman Model. If the test is passed, and the Model is within 18", you can make one Action with it, just as if it were a friendly Model, immediately after This Model's Activation.

Kindred of the Prince: Cost [1], Magic Ability [2]

	Type	Cost	Range	S	Notes
Kindred of the Prince	Magic Buff [2]	1	12"	-	Inspire

Inspire: If successful, the target gains +1 Action in its next Activation.

Lyonesse Ghosts: Cost [1], Magic Ability [4]

	Type	Cost	Range	S	Notes
Lyonesse Ghosts	Projectile	1	12"	3	Gruesome Damage

Affection: Cost [1], Magic Ability [4]

	Type	Cost	Range	S	Notes
Affection	Magic Attack,	1	12"	-	Instant, Confound

Confound: Target enemy living Model makes a Move in a direction chosen by the caster.

Inventors Club

Every Hero Model in the Inventors Club gains a passive ability "Scientist":

Scientist: This Model provides a Control Range for Golems.

Races Available:

Human, Elf, Orc, Troll, Ogre, Gnome, Dwarf and Halfling.

Club Gadgets and Titles

Professions:

Golemologist: Cost [1], suit Spades. Gains Magic Ability [3]: Technomagic and Command spell:

	Type	Cost	Range	S	Notes
Command	Buff [1]	1	12"	-	Command

Command: Choose a Golem within range. The Golem may perform one Action as a part of an extra Activation after Golemologist ends his Activation, then the spell expires.

Technomage: Cost [1], suit Diamonds. Gains Magic Ability [3]: Technomagic and Lightning spell:

	Type	Cost	Range	S	Notes
Lightning	Projectile	0	12"	3	

Engineer: Cost [1], suit Clubs. Gains the Engineer skill:

Engineer: [Quick Action] Once per Activation This Model may use one of the following effects on a friendly Golem in BtB:

• Power Flux: Until the end of turn the Golem icreases its Armor by 2
• Overcharge: Until the end of turn the Golem gains +2 M and +2 S
• Repair: The Golem is immediately restored to its full Wounds

Telekinesis Scholar: Cost [1], suit Hearts. Gains Magic Ability [3]: Technomagic and Shimmer Field spell:

	Type	Cost	Range	S	Notes
Shimmer Field	Aura [2]	1	6"	-	Shield

Shield: Once cast the Field has 10 Wounds and this particular spell cannot be cast by This Model again until the corresponding Field reaches 0 Wounds. Whenever a magical or non-magical Ranged Attack hits a Model within this spell's range the damage is transferred to the Field the Player who controls This Model chooses after adding critical hits but before applying Armor of the targeted Model. If the Field reaches 0 wounds the spell expires. Targeted Model suffers the excess damage as if it was a new attack hitting it once the Field expires.

Gadgets:
Ranged Weapons:

Flagiston Scorcher: [2], Ranged Weapon.

	Strength	0-8"	8-16"	Notes
Flagiston Scorcher	5	„+" 1	-1	Fire, Fire Template

Fire Template: When using this weapon choose a target in range and place the 3" Fire Template completely over it. Make a Ranged Attack against each Model touched by the template then leave it on the battlefield. Models hit suffer a 5 Fire Damage. Remove this template at the end of turn.

Sun Spear: [2], Ranged Weapon.

	Strength	∞"	Notes
Sun Spear	4	„+" 1	Beam

Beam: Beam is special kind of linear Template. When shooting weapon with this rule trace a straight line between This Model and the chosen point in its LoS and continue this in a straight line beyond this point until it no longer is in LoS or reaches the edge of the battlefield. This Model may target all Models in LoS and touched by the Beam Template.

Compact Matter Shifter: [2], Ranged Weapon.

	Strength	0-12"	Notes
Compact Matter Shifter	0	0	Shift

Shift: If you hit the target, instead of causing damage roll a D6 and move Target Model up to the distance rolled in the direction chosen ignoring any terrain. The Model may end this Move in BtB with enemy Model. There must be a place for the Model's base. You may target your own Model with this weapon. In that case target's R is reduced to 0 until end of this Action.

Lab Flask: [1], Ranged Weapon.

	Strength	0-8"	Notes
Lab Flask	0	+ 1	Unintentional result

Melee Weapons:

Mechantric Manipulator: [1], Melee Weapon. Common. +2 S.

Golemic Limb: [2], Melee Weapon. +4 S in Melee

Armor:

Mechanic's Apparel or Lab Suit: [1], Common. Armor [1].

Reflector Field: [1], Armor [3] vs Shooting Attacks.

Spells:

None

[1] cost gadgets

Manic Batteries: [1], Common; Magic Ability [MA] increased by 1.

Manic Amplituner: [1], The Golem control range of equipped Model is increased by 6".

Magneton Boots: [1], May perform Heroic Move or Heroic Recovery without discarding a card. Effects that reduce movement have no effect on the Model regardless of their kind. If a friendly Golem with a larger base starts his Move Action in BtB with the Model equipped with this Gadget after Golem ends its Action you may move the Model to BtB with the Golem.

Personal Phaser: [1], This Model may use this device during his Activation declaring a special Move Action. Mark 3 points anywhere on the table and at least 6" from each other and make a Reflex test. For each success rolled your Opponent nominates a marker that the Model may be placed on facing any direction. If no marker is left - your Opponent chooses the direction and the Model using the device is moved up to his normal Move in the direction chosen. If he contacts any other Model, terrain or the table edge he stops immediately.

Phase Regulator: [1], Once per game. May be used on any friendly Golem in BtB . In its following Activation this turn the Golem may re-roll each and any die during any test it is required to pass.

Stasis Bubble: [1], One use only. Action. Place 3" Stasis Template centered over the Model Activating this Gadget. Until the end of turn no Model may move into the Template and the Model Activating the Gadget is no longer considered as participating in Melee. Models that start their Activation within the Stasis Template must declare a Move Action as their first Action and cannot end their Action inside the area of the Template. Stasis Template does not block LoS or provide cover however any magical or non-magical ranged attack tracing LoS through the marker has its S reduced by 4 to a minimum of 1. If a toppled Model starts its Activation inside the Template it must stand up first and then has to use a Move to leave the Template if it has any Actions left.

Time Warp Generator: [1], Once per game. The Gadget may be used at the beginning of equipped Model's Activation. Until end of turn the Model may perform only Move Actions but doubles its basic M and R.

[2+] cost gadgets:

Golemic Mount: [2], Model's base size becomes 40mm. It has the following rules:

Bash: Models hit by This Model in Melee are Toppled.

Jump: This Model may perform Heroic Move without discarding a card.

Ride [Quick Action] Once per Activation. If This Model starts its Action in BtB with a friendly Model mounted on a 30mm base, it may be placed in BtB with This Model again after This Model Moves. This may cause the placed Model to enter or leave Melee.

Triad of Lotus Dragon

Every Orc Hero Model in the Triad of Lotus Dragon gains a passive ability "Techniques of Sunnir Masters":

Techniques of Sunnir Masters: This Model gains Protection [1] when targeted with enemy spells.

Races Available:

Orc. May have up to one Human, Elf, Troll, Ogre, Gnome, Dwarf and Halfling. You may never have more Heroes of other races than you have Orcs in a Triad club

Triad Gadgets and Professions

Professions:

Stealth Killer: Cost [2], Spades. Gains +1F, +1S and Gruesome Damage in Melee.

Mage: Cost [2], Hearts.Gains Magic Ability [4] and spells Ki Strike and Mistification.

	Type	Cost	Range	Notes
Mistification	Buff [1]	0	6"	Mistwalk

Mistwalk If succesful, Target Model gains Mistwalker this turn.

	Type	Cost	Range	S	Notes
Ki Strike	Projectile	1	12"	6	Topple

Model hit is Toppled.

Blademaster: Cost [1], Diamonds.+1F, Armor Piercing [1] in Melee.

Bodyguard: Cost [0], Clubs. +2W.

Gadgets:

Ranged Weapons:

Firecracker: Cost [3], Ranged Weapon.

	S	0-12"	Notes
Firecracker	4	0	Fire, Instant

Instant: You may use this ability at the end of every Action, even if This Model had made another Action or is in base contact with an enemy Model.

Melee Weapons:

Sabre of the Dragon: Cost [2], Melee Weapon. +3S.

Duellist's Sabre: Cost [3], Melee Weapon. +4F when in base contact with only one enemy Model.

Armor:

Shapeshifter's Tattoos: Cost [2], Armor. At the beginning of This Model's Activation you may choose one of the forms. It suffers the effects of the chosen form until another form is chosen.

Bird: +3M, +3R, -3F, may leave Melee automatically

Snake: +1 F, Gruesome Damage

Elephant: Armor [3], +1S

Armor of Damnation: Cost [4]: Armor. +1 F, +6S, +6W, -1M, -1R, Armor[4]

Cloak of Enshrouding Mists: Cost [2], Armor. Model gains Magic Ability [5] and spells Puppeteer and SpreadingMists:

	Type	Cost	Range	Notes
Puppeteer	Aura [x],	1	12"	Altered Difficulty

Altered Difficulty: Choose a number before casting this spell. This is the spells difficulty. If you succeed the Magic roll, you may choose up to that number of target friendly Models and exchange their places in any combination.

	Type	Cost	Range	Notes
Spreading Mists	Aura [3]	0	12"	Spreading Mists

Spreading Mists: you may place up to 3 Mist Templates within 12" of This Model. Add 3 to the number of available Mist Templates (so counts as 3 more Mistmakers) for the rest of the game. This spell may be only successfully be casted once per game.

Spells:

Staff of the Consuming Darkness: Cost [1], Mages Only. This Model's MA is reduced to 3 and instead of Mistification and Ki Strike This Model knows Leech Soul and Bloodboil spells

	Type	Cost	Range	S	Notes
Leech Soul	Projectile	1	12"	5	Leech

This Model gains Wounds equal to Wounds lost by the Target Model. This model may have more Wounds than it started with.

	Type	Cost	Range	Notes
Bloodboil	Attack/Buff [1]	0	6"	Bloodboil

Bloodboil: Target Model loses 2 W but gains +2S and +2F until end of turn.

[1] cost gadgets:

Mystic Incense: Cost [1], This Model gains <u>Mistmaker:</u> [Quick Action] Place a Mist Template in BtB with This Model

Amulet of Burning Hatred: Cost [1], Models With the Concealed In the Crowd rule within 12" of This Model don't start the game with a Crowd Token. Instead, they have the Gruesome Damage rule.

Despotic Ring: Cost [1], Each Model within 12" of This Model may make a full Activation before the first turn takes place. If a Model does so, he loses half of its wounds, rounding fractions down, at the end of this Activation.

Death Puppet of the Karoa Temple: Cost [1], At the beginning of the game, choose an enemy Hero Model. Whenever that Model loses Wounds, Model with the Death Puppet gains the same amount of Wounds. Whenever This Model loses W, the chosen enemy Model gains that number of W.

Fist of the Tiger: Cost [1], Enemy Models in BtB with This Model never gain Fight bonuses for additional Models in Melee.

Acidic Fumes: Cost[1], Mist Templates within 12" of This Model are Acid Templates instead. Models cannot Mistwalk through these Templates.

[2+] cost gadgets:

Amulet of Life and Death: Cost [2], Whenever another friendly Model within 8" of This Model suffers Damage, put that many Essence Tokens on This Model. Losing Wounds directly is not suffering Damage.

Whenever a friendly Model within 8" of This Model makes a Fight, Guns or Reflex Test, you may remove any number of Essence Tokens to re-roll the same number of dice. The Model performing the Test loses a number of Wounds equal to the number of Essence Tokens removed.

Runic Tattoos: Cost [2], No Model may cast a spell when within 6" of This Model.

BLOCK OF FLATS

WALKWAY

STANDS

WALKWAY

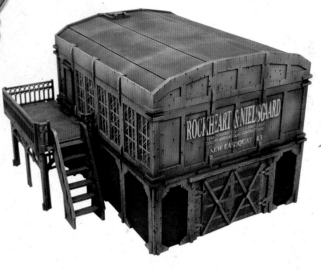

WAREHOUSE

WALL

TOPPLED TOKENS

RSAM COURIER

RSAM COURIER

WOLSUNG DICE

Trattoria

Shantytown

Gaming Mat Streets

Ash and Oak
CLUB STARTERS

Heroes:

Sir Lance Oakroot

Sir Zachary Fiercebatten

Henchmen:

2 Butlers

Ogre Bruiser

The most all-round starter containing both impressive melee skill of Sir Lance and unerring BB gun of Sir Zachary with henchmen for all occassions.

Gameplay: Sir Zachary sits back providing covering fire with one Butler to help him move around while Sir Lance with the other Butler and the Ogre Bruiser engages the enemy up close and personal. Remember to use Sir Lance to tie enemies in melee before you hit them with the Ogre Bruiser, and that Butlers are Hard to Kill as long as Sir Lance is alive!

Good for Clash sized game and beyond.

Heroes:

Mary Fearless

Archibald Armstrong

Henchmen:

House Maid

Ogre Bruiser

Country Cousin

This starter contains more henchmen than the included heroes can afford at once; you will have to choose whether you want to field an Ogre Bruiser or a Country Cousin.

Gameplay: Mary Fearless can engage in shootouts with just about anyone, while Archibald and Ogre Bruiser, thanks to House Maid's healing appearance, can withstand much more damage than Ogres normally would. Alternatively, Country Cousin can provide some long-range high-strength firepower.

This starter really begins to shine at a Brawl or Combat sized game.

Inventors
Club Starters

Heroes:

Alice Tinkerly

Thorvald Nielsgaard

Henchmen:

2 Lab Golems

Lab Assistant

A good all-round starter containing both Alice's Golem-handling abilities and Thorvald's impervious shield to protect your team. On top of that tough and disposable henchmen that are able to handle most battlefield situations.

Gameplay: These models need to stick together. Thorvald provides protection from firearms while Alice assists the Golems to get into place. Use chokepoints to control who can attack your Heroes. Golems need to tank at the front while both the Heroes can come into the melee later and deliver a staggering blow. The Lab Assistant is the only truly free moving model here and he may be able to escape the attention for long enough to throw the game-changing Nitrogliceryne-filled flask into the middle of the enemy lines.

Good for Clash sized game and beyond.

Heroes:

Stephany Seagull

Professor Egir Eldstrom

Henchmen:

2 Lab Assistants

Biocognitator Golem

This is a more advanced starter. Egir makes the Lab Assistants much more reliable and with a total of 3 Lab-flask throwing models it is not going to be a dry shiny day for your opponent.

Gameplay: Stephany Seagull should hang back and try to carpet the way for the Biocognitator Golem with Golem Beacons, either on enemy models, friendly Lab Assistants, or even Egir. You don't really need to use your cards for Hero abilities so they can be spent to make Biocognitator take control over the world. Remember that you can throw a lab flask at Egir to enrage him.

This starter really starts to shine at a Brawl or Combat sized game.

Triad of Lotus Dragon
CLUB STARTERS

Heroes:

Xen Jidao

Phoenix

Henchmen:

Trader

Fisherman

Shadow

A good all-round starter containing all the basic tools in the Triad's arsenal: the heavy hitter Phoenix and the key to Mistwalking Xen, plus Mistmaking Traders and a Fisherman for toppling crucial enemy models.

Gameplay: Advance with the Traders on both flanks spreading mists while Fisherman positions himself to Topple the most dangerous enemy model just prior to the engagement. Keep Phoenix and Xen back and make use of Xen's Mistwalk spell to transport Phoenix where most needed. Do not forget that Xen's Ki Strike spell also Topples.

Good for Clash sized game, starts to really shine at a Brawl sized game and beyond.

Heroes:

Mr Cheng

Hisao Shiryo

Henchmen:

3 Golemic Dragonlings

Onryo

The most fiendish and hard to use starter that can kill enemies by Mist, Acid, Magic, or brute force.

Gameplay: There are a lot of interactions between abilities here. Golemic Dragonlings and Hisao can Mistwalk, yet within 12" of Mr Cheng there is no Mistwalking. The Mist within this area turns into Acid, dealing damage, but the Dragonlings and Onryo have Sour Sustenance. Mr Cheng really shines when he Leeches enough souls to have more than 21 Wounds, but he also can just cast Bloodboil on Dragonlings and Onryo and make their Sour Sustenance mitigate the lost wounds. Then Hisao can move Acidic Mists or summon the Horrors of the Aether… out of Acidic Mists.

Good for Clash sized game, starts to really shine at a Brawl sized game and beyond.

WOLSUNG
Steampunk Skirmish Game

ON THE WEB

WOLSUNG-SSG.COM
SHOP.MICROARTSTUDIO.COM

Engage in a rules or game related discussion with other players and game developers on our forum. Show your painted models and creations, ask for modelling advice, write and read battlereports!

wolsung-ssg.com/forum

We have provided a tool to create your custom characters for Wolsung SSG. Head to our website and click Hero Creator! This app will generate a card for your Hero to print out and play with.

wolsung-ssg.com/herocreator

Follow Wolsung SSG on Facebook, Twitter and Youtube to see and discuss latest releases:

 /WolsungSSG   @WolsungSSG   /microartstudio01

Index

114

INDEX

119